A Gratitude for Time

Understanding Your Relationships with Time

By
Suresh Eswaran

A Gratitude for Time:
Understanding Your Relationships with Time

Cover Design By: Kenneth Jordan of JG Graphics
Edited By: Sarajoy Bonebright
www.gratitudeforTime.com

Table of Contents

About the Author

"I wonder if I've been changed in the night. Let me think. Was I the same when I got up this morning? I almost think I can remember feeling a little different. But if I'm not the same, the next question is 'Who in the world am I?' Ah, that's the great puzzle!"
— *Lewis Carroll, <u>Alice in Wonderland</u>*

The simplified version is: I was born in 1992 in Sacramento, California. By age 3, I had a tennis racquet in my hand, and for the next 20 years, I was a tennis player and spent a majority of my life on or around a tennis court.

I played in the South Eastern Conference (SEC) and graduated from Vanderbilt University in 2015. After graduating, I decided I didn't enjoy tennis enough to try to make a living becoming a professional—a funny realization to make after 20 years, but definitely not uncommon and not limited to tennis. However, I struggled to define who I was separate of the sport I had played my entire life.

Eventually I realized that I wasn't just a tennis player, but also a friend, son, brother, human being, and more. Once I grew through the disorder of my identity crisis and created a sense of inner peace; I had a new (good) problem. I had no idea what I wanted to do with my life, given the near infinite amount of possibilities that were now open in my future.

One day I was feeling entrepreneurial, was considering some business ideas, and asked myself the question, *What do people need?*

At some point, the thought came across my mind that people needed Time.

It seemed to hold true in any case that I could think of, but I quickly realized I had no idea what Time was or why it was true that people needed it.

Since 2015, I have been researching and learning about the concept of Time from various perspectives, including physics, mathematics, logic, biology, philosophy, sociology, history, psychology, quantum mechanics, neuroscience, and mental health.

As it applies to individual humans, I have observed that when a human faces the reality that their Time is finite and that death is an ever-increasing probability, they desire 3 things most from Time: a sense of **meaning, happiness, and purpose** in their life.

What I have observed and become aware of on larger scales is that how we value Time as individuals and societies largely determines the quality of our subjective experience of life—our relationships to ourselves, our relationships to other people, and, even more crucially, our relationships to nature and technology.

Unfortunately, most cultures, especially modern western culture, influence billions of people to undervalue Time and overvalue money. This is one of the problems I hope to raise awareness of with this book.

If nothing else, I hope that you gain some power and awareness of *your* Time by realizing how valuable and finite Time is for all of us living things and how that makes all life different *and* similar, *simultaneously*.

General Opening Thoughts

Read Time: 3 minutes of attention

"Whatever comes out of these gates, we've got a better chance of survival if we work together. Do you understand? If we stay together, we survive."

— _Maximus (The Gladiator)_

Don't you think it's funny that, literally, for every second of your life, you have had a relationship with Time? And you may be realizing right now that this is, has, and will always be the case, for as long as you live.

Yet how often have you wondered or thought to figure out what it is that you are spending? What does it mean to spend Time?

What does it mean to "do Time"? What is it that prisoners must give up when they have been convicted of a crime?

What are you wasting when you waste Time?

Time is not a topic of discussion just for theoretical physicists, grandparents, or mathematicians; it is a relevant and urgent issue for everyone right now, especially during the era of automation, artificial intelligence, and climate change.

These questions and more will be explored in this book. You might discover that learning about Time isn't just about learning about Time; it's learning about yourself, human beings, the world around you, and most especially learning about reality.

Don't let fear or complexity deter you from thinking longer about Time. That's what this book is for: to provide a safe path into the unknown so that you can explore and learn about one of the most important ideas our minds have access to.

The future is not predictable nor controllable, but it is influence-able. We have already entered a new geologic era called the "Anthropocene" Era. It is characterized by human influence on Earth, specifically climate change due to industrialization, increasing population, and the development of fossil fuel dependent large-scale cities.

While quality of life is improving, as compared to past generations, what people seem to be paying attention to, thinking, and reacting to is *negativity* in a variety of forms. This purveyance of negativity can be thought of as a form of chronic stress on a population, group, team, or species.

Our relationships to ourselves, technology, each other, and nature all hinge on our ability to unconsciously and consciously value Time properly, especially in relation to money.

Whatever happens in the future, we need to take Maximus's advice. We will only survive... we will only *cultivate* happiness and systemic peace... if we work together.

How to Read This Book

Feel free to read this book however you want—from beginning to end or hopping around sections over Time—whatever best fits in with your schedule, your ability to pay attention, and your interests, curiosities, wants, and/or needs. However, if you enjoy recommendations, mine would be to take it in *small* doses, over 3-6 months.

It's important to note that each topic is its own section, and the book is not written to be read with each chapter connected sequentially. The chapters are connected to each other, and to you, through the concept of Time. The chapters do not necessarily flow into each other like a typical story, so there is no harm in bouncing around or picking it up again after a few weeks. Maybe a chapter a day would work best for you.

To gain the most value, it probably will be best to set your ego aside and try to hold an objective perspective of what you read— not necessarily believing or disbelieving anything immediately, but testing it against your own experiences and logic and seeing if it holds true.

I have purposely capitalized the word "Time" throughout this book. I didn't do it to confuse you; I did this so that you would be consciously and unconsciously influenced to value Time differently—also so that you start to realize that Time is something far greater than something that you measure on a clock or watch.

Lastly, I did it to help get you out of your own way and to move past your preconceived ideas of what Time may or may not be.

You will be surprised how many different ways the same word and concept can be used in language and in our everyday lives.

While you read, I recommend taking notes, either handwritten or typed, of your thoughts, feelings, and ideas. You will find that this will help you to better mold the information you learn to your own realities that you experience.

Our Relationship with Time

Read Time: 11 minutes of attention

---

*"Literally every moment
of your life is captured in Time."*

– S.E.

You and I have very interesting and many different relationships with Time. In one sense, we are Time. Our whole lives are the sum of all the seconds we spend mentally and physically, consciously and unconsciously. As far as we can understand, we are indeed spending Time every moment of our lives. Not just that, but we are spending a majority of our Time *unconsciously*.

Each of our bodily organs and even cells have their own "local" Times that must synchronize with each other in one way or another for our sense of self to exist—an aspect of our biological relationship with Time.

In another sense, Time is what allows for the possibility of life, and it is the main reason why we eventually die. It's both the giver and taker of life. Here we have a philosophical and/or psychological relationship with Time.

As individuals, the psychological relationship is where we have the most influence and control. As a collective, we are making leaps and bounds in figuring out how to influence the human biological body and spend a lot of money trying to find solutions that optimize and elongate our health.

We have a biological understanding of "self", as a boundary of matter moving amongst a world of matter. This is primitive, in that an insect has this sense of self. Our more sophisticated sense of self comes from our minds and has evolved with our ability to perceive new forms of Time as well.

Who are you? Technically, there is no right answer, because the answer is always in a state of change. You are always in a state of change as each second passes. You have to consider unconscious biological functions, like producing new skin cells every 30 days or so, not to forget a multitude of unconscious processes that are in motion at any given moment, like learning, understanding, or growing.

"You" are not one thing. In fact, understandings derived from quantum mechanics show us that there is no such thing as a "thing"—only relationships.

Saint Augustine, described the self as 3 selves that were in a constant state of change: your present-past self, present-present self, and present-future self.

What he meant by this, and I agree with, is that because we are constrained to only a "present moment" at a Time, we can only have a "right now" image of who we were, who we are, and who we will be. All three are constantly in a state of change, and over Time, we sense these changes and see ourselves as different.

Who you believe you were, who you are, and who you will be, at the age of 10, is most probably very different than who you believe you were, who you are, and who you will be, at age 20, 30, 40, 50, and so on.

Every human and every living thing has a relationship with Time. This relationship makes us all alike at the most fundamental level, but when we pay closer attention, we find incredible diversity that has grown from common, simple rules.

Universal 6th Sense

Read Time: 13 minutes of attention

"We tend to assume Time is the same for everyone, but according to research published in the journal <u>Animal Behaviour</u>, it has different speeds for different species."

— Russell McClendon, Mother Nature Network

Most of us are familiar with our traditional 5 senses and the body parts associated with those senses. For those of you who have forgotten, here is a reminder: Ears (hearing), hands (touch), nose (smell), eyes (sight), and tongue (taste). Our senses allow us to interact and gather information about the world outside of our bodies.

But where does Time fit into all of this?

We all know someone with a bad sense of Time, who is always late to everything or misses appointments. Some people are known to have a good sense of Time; they show up to everything on Time or early.

Some people have great timing; some people have bad timing. The fact that those are understandable and familiar characteristics is what I am driving at. We do, in fact, have a *sense* of Time.

We track Time in various parts of our brain and body, which all interact to integrate a variety of informational inputs that we receive on a second-to-second basis. This incredible ability to integrate, interpret, and use temporal information is not unique to humans. Many species, if not all, are known to have a sense of

Time. Even trees and plants have a sense of Time that oscillates around the changing of seasons.

How is it that dogs know when their owners are returning from work? Or that it's the Time of day to eat or go for a walk? It's not as if each of our dogs secretly has smartphones with timers or schedules set up for them. There are various biological and environmental factors at play.

Birds migrate only during certain periods during the year. Sharks know it's best to hunt seals during their mating season, which describes a sense of Time on both the part of the sharks and seals. These examples point to the fact that Time is at least an inherent biological phenomenon. I'd like to illustrate one of the most important things about Time that has been described in each example.

Time is primarily about our relationship with other things and people. Dogs are able to orient around their human owners, and humans around their dogs. Birds orient around other birds. Sharks orient around seals, and vice versa.

Despite having very different bodily structures and a variety of senses, Time is prevalent across all kinds of brains, bodies, and minds.

I call Time, the "universal 6th sense", because by nature of living on Earth and being in the Milky Way Galaxy, humans and almost all life must interact and maintain relationships using Time.

Humans like to think of themselves as all powerful and sophisticated, but our primal instincts still control and influence us on a day-to-day basis and over the course of our lifetimes. Our sense of Time is vital to being able to survive, succeed, and enjoy life together on a finite world with finite Time.

Time, the Trickster

Read Time: 5 minutes of attention

---

*"The first principle is to not fool yourself—and you
are the easiest person to fool."*
– Richard Feynman

This book is an attempt to help push forward humanity's collective knowledge surrounding the concept of Time. I believe that individually and collectively this is the first obstacle to addressing imminent global issues, such as climate change, political conflicts, human migrations, wealth/power gaps, unnecessary suffering, unhappiness, and other forms of disorder.

So, then, what is Time? It is many things, but for starters, Time is a trickster.

It not only plays tricks on us individually, but also on all of us simultaneously, as a collective. Time's greatest trick is to fool Homo sapiens ("wise men") into making us think, believe, and act as if Time wasn't our most valuable resource—logically, biologically, and mathematically.

How does Time play this trick? By disguising "gold" as "pennies". Time flows so continuously, seamlessly, and predictably, day after day, year after year, and generation after generation, that it's very easy to take it for granted and forget that our Time here is extremely temporary. If Time is seen as a measurable currency, through which we pay for life, then Time is tricking us into thinking that seconds have the value of a penny, when they really have the value of gold (if not more, actually).

11

What I hope you get out of this is that each second is inherently valuable, because the sum of your Time spent is literally your life. It is also true though that not all moments have the same value. In this perspective, Time is life.

Timescales

Read Time: 2 minutes of attention

"Timescales allow us to see the changing world as it is changing, sometimes before it has changed."

– S.E.

Timescales, as I am going to introduce them here, are just an easy way to visualize how Time is embedded into every aspect of everything and everyone we interact with. Timescales allow us to see past, present, and future all at once. They allow us to engage in timing and influence outcomes in our futures.

Timescales are simply the length of Time a living organism, event, idea, thing, object, planet, and process have existed in Time, *measured against* another scale of Time.

Oddly enough, we do this unconsciously, mapping everything against Time itself. Concepts of "old" and "new" arise from this mapping process.

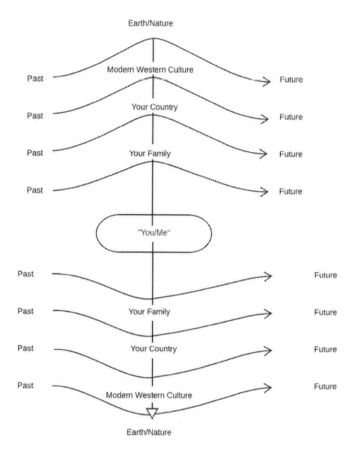

One aspect the figure displays is how Earth influences each of us and how, over Time, we influence Earth. In the same way, our families influence us, and over Time, we influence our families. The scale and degree of this influence varies, depending on what you are paying attention to, but the general principles still apply.

Another aspect of the figure shows that while each of us have our own lifetime or timescale, so too does Earth and our families. If we die, Time and reality still unfold without missing a beat.

The structure in the image is also very flexible and moldable. Depending on your realities and what you pay attention to or value, you could add any timescales. Millions, if not billions, of timescales could be mapped; don't limit yourself.

Each human represents a timescale—with birth as their starting point and death as their ending point, at some unknown point in the future. Having estimates of when something started or ended is more than enough.

Timescales outside of humans include nature; a river has a timescale, which viewed in its entirety would describe how it has changed and grown into what we see with our eyes in that "present moment"—in essence, describing the "life" of the river. This can be done with birds, alligators, mountains, buildings, trees, cars, and even city infrastructures.

Intangible things, like ideas, can also have timescales, although they usually have more general approximations in Time, regarding the "beginning and ends" of their timescale.

The concept of timescales allows the mind to perceive of future Time and how, to a degree, to foresee how people and things will interact, based upon the little and incomplete information we have and upon what we pay attention to in our own individual lives.

In Time, We Gamble

Read Time: 25 minutes of attention

"The subject of gambling is all encompassing. It combines man's natural play instinct with his desire to know his fate and his future"

— Franz Rosenthal

Life is very much about navigating uncertainty; however it may be manifesting in our subjective experiences. Based upon our limited frame of reference (our subjective experience of the world/reality) throughout Time, uncertainty is pretty much stitched into every second of our operating lives. We can't predict or control every aspect of our lives; we have to live with uncertainty. I think that is what makes life so exciting and scary.

Uncertainty underlies almost every single decision we make, big or small—from walking across the street to choosing the person you're going to marry.

The following is a brief explanation of why uncertainty always surrounds us:

From what I understand about quantum mechanics, the future is inherently unpredictable. It used to be believed that the future was fixed or determined, but that has been found not to be the case. The most we can do is calculate probabilities, and even that gets difficult the further out into the future you try to predict. The reason for the unpredictability of the future is because there are so many factors that have to be accounted for—so many possibilities that have a .001% or lower chance of occurring.

The crazy thing is that there are a billion different outcomes that have a .001% probability, and that means improbable things are bound to occur far more often than we can properly predict. Random, nearly-impossible events can lead to other random, nearly-impossible events, and in this way, we just have to move away from trying to predict or control the future.

Physicists have tried to predict the future, even at the microscopic level; they have shot photons (small particles/waves of light) through a pathway and tried to predict where they would end up. The most they could do was say that 96% of photons would end up in one place and 4% would end up somewhere else, but they couldn't say which photons would go where. Every Time they ran the experiment, the probability held true, but they could not specify which photon would travel where. In other words, they could not predict how reality would unfold; they could only give the probability that certain outcomes would occur.

I'm sure you have experienced many improbable occurrences in your own life, and if you pay attention, you'll notice them more frequently now. Unfortunately, most people do not properly account for uncertainty in their decision-making. By nature, we are more driven by our fears than by our dreams, which comes from our biological desire to survive.

However, some of our evolutionary tools are not as useful as they were 10,000 years ago. The world is changing much faster than the "slow" pace of evolution, and survival and reproduction are not necessarily the primary drivers of human life today.

I would argue that living a meaningful, purposeful, and happy life is the emerging primary goal that humanity is moving towards now and in the near future.

If I haven't put you to sleep already, I'd like to shift away from physics and transition to a philosophical perspective briefly.

Again, uncertainty underlies every decision we make, and it has to do with the fact that there are factors that influence our destiny that are outside of our control. This takes us back to death.

Every day when you wake up, you have a small chance of dying—whether this be by accident, choking on a cherry, getting hit by a drunk driver, heart failure, etc. This may sound obvious, and it is. However, there is a difference between accepting these realities and making decisions with them in mind.

The reason I am telling you this is because it points to the fact that Time is unpredictable and largely out of our control. Paradoxically, accepting our powerlessness, immediately empowers us to greatly reduce risk in living happier, meaningful, and purposeful lives.

Biology and Time

Read Time: 16 minutes of attention

"When a man is asleep, he has in a circle round him the chain of the hours, the sequence of the years, the order of the heavenly bodies. Instinctively he consults them when he awakens and in an instant reads off his own position on the Earth's surface and the Time that has elapsed during his slumbers."

– Proust

In 2017, the Nobel Prize for physiology and medicine was awarded to a team that discovered how our internal bodies use sunlight to control our circadian rhythms, below conscious awareness.

Our sleep, hormones, diet, and energy cycles are influenced greatly by this process and triggered by the relationship with Earth's revolution around the Sun.

Every day when you wake up, your body is orienting and reorienting itself in space and Time (spacetime). Your brain and body have to set in motion unconscious biological and chemical processes inside your body to keep you functioning. For example, *you* are not the one consciously telling your body to raise energy levels in the morning, so you can go about your day, and then to lower your energy levels at night so you can sleep.

Even though we don't control those processes consciously, we can help influence them simply by being consistent and accepting the fact that there are larger things in this world than our individual selves that we have to align to. The relationship between the Sun

21

and Earth is one of those larger influences. Simply having a personal rhythm that is closer to the rhythm of the sunrise and sunset has shown to reduce the risk of various diseases and improve mental health over Time.

Even though I do a bad job of it myself, it is important to not look at smartphones or other devices right before bed. You're in essence fooling your body and messing with your circadian rhythm and alignment with Earth's rotation and timing. Over Time, this throws off energy levels, creates chemical imbalances, and other inconsistencies or misalignments that negatively affect our bodies, minds, and experiences of Time.

Aging is a well-known relationship between our bodies and Time. We know, as we get older and older, our bodies are slowly deteriorating. What we were able to easily physically do as a teenager, or a 28-year-old, becomes far more difficult at age 50+.

As a freshman and sophomore in college, I could stay out until 2am and then wake up three hours later at 5:30am to go run sprints with my teammates for tennis practice. During the beginning of my junior year, I tried to do this, and the next morning, it felt like a garbage truck ran over me.

I quickly realized that my body was no longer able to process alcohol and produce energy in ways that my younger self had the privilege of. I had to make a decision to change my habits and stay in on nights that I had anything productive to do the next morning.

By becoming aware of our physical relationship with Time, we can be more adaptable to what our bodies tell us and spend our Time in a way that allows us to optimize our energy and attention as individuals. When I say "optimize", I don't just mean efficiency; I also mean enjoyment. Not everything is about speed. It is far easier to enjoy life when we feel like we are full of energy and our bodies are rested.

Athletes, like Lebron James and Tom Brady, have seemingly reduced the effects of Time (aging) by prioritizing proper rest. It doesn't take millions of dollars to have good rest and high energy, but it does take self-awareness and self-love to prioritize your own health and listen to what your body needs and when.

The Mind and Time

Read Time: 24 minutes of attention

"As far as the human mind can fathom, for Life to be possible, Time must pass."

– S.E.

Modern science and knowledge have shown us that our minds are not only incredibly valuable and powerful, but also very complex. Leading scientists in neuroscience, psychology, and consciousness are still unsure of how the mind truly works, and they aren't that close to coming to a unified understanding. One aspect of the mind that has been overlooked and that can provide valuable insight into the inner workings of the mind is the mental relationship with Time.

If your friend accidentally hits their head, and in the process of assessing if they are okay, they tell you it's the year 1919, you automatically know something is wrong. It doesn't take an expert to know that how we orient ourselves in Time determines our perception of reality.

Our minds use Time to structure reality, to perceive our own "selves", to create and store memories, to interact in society, and to otherwise simply make sense of the universe and life. The mind is both influenced by Time and also does the influencing.

Unlike our bodies, the mind is not as strictly bound by Time. Our mind can move fluidly between past, present, and future. This is both a blessing and a burden. It's a blessing because we have immense influence over how we use our own Time, how we structure it, the meaning we give it, and what we decide to build/create with it.

With our minds, we can reflect and learn from the past; we can engage in a state of flow and enjoy the present (regardless of what we are doing); or we can look out into the future and invest to achieve higher ROI's (return on investment) on the Time that we will hopefully get to spend.

However, a lot of this power is wasted or lost due to the fact that most people have little awareness or control over when/where their mind goes. Without consistent practice and effort, the mind will drift from the present moment, like a lost balloon floating into the sky. All the while, seconds and moments still tick by, and life will literally pass you, without you even realizing it. For the most part your smartphone and the social media apps we engage with, are hurting your attentional abilities rather than helping them.

Academically, it's called mind wandering, and it often occurs during work for most people. It can even contribute to dissatisfaction with or at work. Apparently, mind wandering can also occur for a lot of women during sex.

Albert Einstein discovered, from a physics perspective, what the mind can do to Time. He called it relativity, but a lot of us understand the term "subjective experience" better.

Whether on purpose or by context, our minds can manipulate the feeling of Time. One minute can feel like an hour, and one hour can feel like a minute. Objectively the same amount of Time still passes, but subjectively that experience and feeling is unique to us (the observer or measurer). I won't get too far into the details, but it does make you wonder how two or more people can feel like it's been a long week or a short year.

What Time Really Is

Read Time: 8 minutes of attention

"What is time then?
If no one asks me, I know what it is.
If I wish to explain it to him who asks,
I do not know."
— *Saint Augustine*

Like Augustine, I cannot provide you with an all-encompassing answer, but I can provide several true answers that are verifiable.

Time is one of the most flexible and scalable ideas our minds have access to. In one perspective, Time can be seen as an element of our habitat, not just physically, but mentally as well.

Time provides the foundational structure upon which reality unfolds. We know this from the 2nd Law of Thermodynamics. It tells us that Time passes from past → future, and that disorder/entropy increases in correlation with Time passing.

For those who don't believe or agree with science, we can prove the existence of Time in other ways. If you believe you live on planet Earth and that the Sun exists, you must also believe that the entirety of your life takes place within Time and can be conceptually measured in seconds on a 24-hour grid.

Don't be overwhelmed though, we are just publicly agreeing on something we all knew already and acted upon our entire lives. For some reason, humans love unspoken rules and agreements, but this encourages us to live inside our own minds rather than being present and experiencing each moment of life as it actually is.

Our concept of Time that we are most familiar with—clock Time or Universal Coordinated Time (UTC)—is born in the relationship between the Sun and Earth. It started with the observation of the cycles between night and day and evolved into the grid-like structure we know as our *days and hours*. Through UTC, we measure Time through various symbolic instruments including, but not limited to:

1. Clocks (digital + analog)
2. Calendars
3. Schedules
4. Reminders
5. Alarms
6. Watches

Time is also the measurement of relationships. Just as we can measure Time by observing the relationship between the Sun and Earth, we can measure and learn about Time from exploring the relationship between "things".

Societies and cultures have existed in relation to mountain ranges, wars, leaders, eras of peace, natural disasters, and almost anything else that has made it to our human-created histories. Whether it be between subatomic particles, human beings, ideas, values, or any combination that you could think of, Time exists in relation to other things.

By exploring our relationship to Time, we are also exploring ourselves—who we were, who we are, and who we are becoming.

Time and Work

Read Time: 15 minutes of attention

"You will never feel truly satisfied by work until you are satisfied by life."
— Heather Schuck,
The Working Mom Manifesto

Over ⅓ of our life is spent working. Our relationship with our "work" is incredibly important and influential to our perception of life, simply based on the percentage of Time spent under that category.

Given the capabilities of technology and automation, hard work is becoming less valuable than smart work. We can do and create things far faster than we could even just 20 years ago.

As a collective, we are gaining access to massive amounts of free Time. Basically, this means that we are gaining power over what we do with our Time and why. We will need to transition away from salary being our primary decision-making factor, to a more reality-based decision-making process.

This process starts with consideration for how we would spend our Time and who we would spend our Time around. Salary and monetary value come into consideration *after* those 2 criteria have been satisfied. Satisfying the first two criteria dramatically increases your *probability* of securing and cultivating a sense of meaning, happiness, and purpose in that job.

Work generally is important to us because we derive a majority of our meaning and sense of purpose from work. Millennials are starting to bring to attention the human need to align individual meaning and purpose to our company's meaning and purpose. This includes some degree and scale of alignment with our bosses, peers, and teams.

Work is not just a way to make some money; it can be much more. Work provides opportunities to cultivate skills, build and engage in our various communities, learn new things about ourselves and the world, create value through products or services, make money, cultivate meaning and purpose, build a "career", travel, cultivate individual and collective happiness, help people, and much more.

Whatever your definition of work is, you will have to be more aware and ready to identify and make good use of your free Time. We are gaining more and more of it every year. How we use our free Time, individually and collectively, is literally going to determine our futures and your future.

A Dose of Reality: Death

Read Time: 16 minutes of attention

"Remembering that I'll be dead soon is the most important tool I've ever encountered to help me make the big choices in life."

– Steve Jobs

Please do not be afraid to think about your own mortality and temporariness. Paradoxically, accepting the reality of death is actually incredibly freeing and adds immense positive value and meaning to your Time.

For a perfectly healthy young and happy adult, the probability of dying each day is incredibly small. But there is a probability, and the chance is always greater than zero. There are so many uncontrollable and unpredictable factors that could impact whether we die, or not, on a daily basis.

For example, no one plans to get hit by a drunk driver while crossing the street, but statistically it happens every day to someone. War is another scenario in which many uncontrollable factors can determine whether someone lives or dies. Cancer is another example that has affected millions of people, whether it directly claimed their life or not.

However, it doesn't even need to be that dramatic; simple accidents occur every day to everyday people. As an individual, the possibility of death is present each and every day.

From a longer perspective, say 100 years, the probability of dying skyrockets to nearly 100%. Who was the last person you personally knew that lived to be over 100 years old? It is far more common to know those who have died before even reaching the age of 30.

It's surprisingly sad and disturbing how much death and poverty is attributed to greed, the pursuit of profit, ego, securing power, and other negative human motivations..

Many people try to make the argument that modern science is improving our ability to live longer and possibly even skirt death altogether. It is true that at the forefront of modern science there are great innovations to help reduce the effects of aging and biological deterioration, but those treatments are probably not going to be easily accessible to the public for many years and will probably only affordable by the very wealthy.

Even if everyone had access to these kinds of innovations, do you think it is likely you will live for the next billion years? Probably not. Would you even want to live forever? I would argue fear would mostly motivate you to say yes.

The picture I am painting is not positive, nor is it negative. It simply is an illustration of an embedded aspect of reality. Each day we live, we have a chance of dying, and the more days we are alive, that probability increases non-linearly until one day it reaches certainty.

This may seem somewhat obvious to you, but it is surprising how many people deny the inevitable reality of their deaths,. We cannot just assume other people know and act upon this knowledge; we have to tangibly agree and say it out loud to each other and to ourselves.

People make small and big decisions with no real consideration for the fact that they may die or that the people they love may die, and this hurts their own ability to lead happy, meaningful, and purposeful lives.

Every once in a while considering death can be good, because it forces you to acknowledge the reality that your Time is finite. It directs focus and awareness to the deep desire to live a meaningful, purposeful, and happy life.

I am not trying to preach to you how to live; I'm simply saying that there are certain restrictions on how you can spend your Time, that your Time is finite, and that when embracing the reality of death, you are more empowered to influence your own happiness, meaning, and purpose in life.

Cultivating Human Happiness

Read Time: 30 minutes of attention

"For most of life, nothing wonderful happens. If you don't enjoy getting up and working and finishing your work and sitting down to a meal with family or friends, then the chances are you're not going to be very happy. If someone bases their happiness on major events like a great job, huge amounts of money, a flawlessly happy marriage, or a trip to Paris, that person isn't going to be happy much of the Time. If, on the other hand, happiness depends on a good breakfast, flowers in the yard, a drink or a nap, then we are more likely to live with quite a bit of happiness."
— *Andy Rooney*

Unfortunately, the idea of happiness has been unclear and warped throughout history. In the last couple hundred years, the idea of happiness has been largely distorted by politics and economics and by the desire for power and efficiency—all of which have been accelerated through the advertising industry.

Luckily, today, there is plenty of research in biology, physics, neuroscience, psychology, and well-being to give us a much more objective and scalable understanding of what happiness is and how to grow it for ourselves as individuals, communities, and as a species that influences all other forms of life.

The first obstacle is coming to the understanding that happiness is something that is cultivated not pursued. Happiness is cultivated within the mind, by each of us using and investing Time—literally spending and investing real seconds that you are or will most likely spend.

Below is a modern definition of happiness, scalable to every human on Earth.

35

Human happiness = One's contentment with how they spend their Time, mentally and physically.

Mental Time is simply the Time, or the string of seconds that your mind spends. Physical Time is represented by the string of seconds your body spends. These two timescales are connected, but not necessarily aligned. In fact, for many they are misaligned often.

Easy examples are shown when people drive and let their mind wander, or when physically at work but thinking about an upcoming vacation.

Mental Time is parallel to *attention.* It is useful to use mental Time, because then attention can become measurable. So we can then direct and influence attention by investing and spending mental Time.

Physical Time is important because we experience and live our lives through our precious and incredibly intelligent bodies. What we do with them matters to us and matters to the people and world around us. Our bodies also influence our minds and vice versa.

Throughout human history, people have desired a sense of happiness in their lives. Aristotle even proclaimed that happiness is the end goal to which the entirety of our lives aim.

The following is a universal process for cultivating human happiness, based on research from neuroscience, well-being, and positive psychology:

Human happiness is cultivated over the course of Time, by spending and investing Time in four ways:

1. <u>Consistently spend and invest physical and mental Time into your human relationships.</u>

   Our human relationships are one of the biggest influences on our happiness and unhappiness. If we don't feel connected to others and to our communities, we may quickly believe we are isolated and alone, and we may enter a painful and avoidable cycle of suffering, among other possible negative mental and physical outcomes.

When we feel connected to others, the positive outcomes are numerous. We are better at facing reality because we feel safe. We share resources better and are better able to make larger amounts of money through trust. We are happier, physically more active, and healthier; our children are happier and safer; and as a society, country, and species, we are more prosperous and better able to thrive. We even live longer when we focus on building positive relationships with the humans around us.

2. Consistently spend and invest physical and mental Time into your own self growth.

    One purpose of life (all life) is to grow. Not only that, but our brains and minds actually improve in function if we continuously learn new things and improve upon our skills.

    For our brains, our synapses are strengthened and exercised, which is important for cognitive health and performance over Time. For the mind, our sense of self-confidence, joy, and curiosity all increase when we have a growth mindset. (google Carol Dweck's work.) There is so much variety to what we can consider self-growth, and we as individuals need to figure out what works best for us.

3. Consistently spend and invest physical and mental Time helping others.

    This one is similar to the first category; however, it puts a focus on thinking outside of yourself and bringing value to others—friends or strangers. Donating money to some foundation is good and helpful, but it's not a strong nor sustainable way to invest in your own happiness.

Giving others your Time is giving part of your life to enhance another's life. It's a very gratifying feeling and experience, and most, if not all, of us have experienced it one way or another already.

Simply holding the door for someone else or giving your Time to someone who is struggling is far more beneficial to your own sense of happiness than donations through social media.

From this perspective, collective happiness is attainable through individual selfishness, because to be selfish in this model is to help others.

4. <u>Consistently spend and invest physical and mental Time into creating, updating, and acting upon your values and beliefs.</u>

Your values and beliefs influence how you think, speak, decide, and act over the course of Time. Most of our Time spent in life is spent unconsciously, and by taking the Time to rewrite and encode our own values and beliefs, we gain power to influence how we will unconsciously be and grow over Time.

If you don't constantly reevaluate your values and beliefs, you can get "stuck in the past". More accurately, you begin to lose your ability to adapt to reality.

Periodic evaluation of values and beliefs is the difference between two people who grew up in Virginia in 1900. Both grew up with the belief that white skin is more valuable than colored skin. Over Time, societal beliefs were challenged and changed, but for the individuals, they had choices to make.

Person A is able to update his values and beliefs, question their validity, and form a new belief that is based on modern science and human knowledge.

Person B rejects cultural changes and scientific knowledge updates—thus embedding himself further into an older belief that was most likely created for the preservation of economic power and hierarchy by a few humans.

Person B lives in a world misaligned with his inner world and is far more likely to be unhappy, bitter, and isolated from the rest of society.

Person A is able to adapt and survive in a highly volatile and uncertain world and increase the probability of inner happiness and peace.

The point here is not to simply conform to the majority but to genuinely determine what we value and believe throughout Time.

Consciously question your own values and beliefs so that you can authentically live your life and stay adaptable to new information and knowledge. Time changes, reality changes, life changes, our values change, and our beliefs change.

For most of us, our values and beliefs are instilled in childhood by our parents, friends, culture, and other influences. This process of evaluating and renewing our values and beliefs can be a painful growth process, but it is necessary if we want to know ourselves or have any real sense of control over ourselves.

Life Is Simultaneously Meaningless and Meaningful

Read Time: 40 minutes of attention

"Those who have a 'why' can endure any 'how'. I encourage every human to go beyond finding, and create their own 'whys'."

– Nietzsche

We live in a mathematical and objective universe. Reality is a cold place that doesn't account for our feelings, hopes, desires, or fears. It simply unfolds over Time. The laws of physics are evidence to this. Things happen because they were possible or probable, or became possible or probable, not because they were meant to.

Our brains and minds are designed to construct narratives from all the information that we intake constantly over Time. After attaching meaning to our past, present, or future, we then believe these meanings and narratives. This occurs subconsciously or unconsciously for most of us.

Despite the involuntariness of this process, the narratives and meanings we attach to our Time further influence us on a moment-to-moment basis—influencing how we perceive ourselves, how we treat others, how we perceive the world around us, our decisions, habits, and in general our lives.

This is to say, that the meaning we subjectively attach to Time is meaningful to us. Our narratives are important to us, and they should be taken into consideration when considering a human

41

being, *because who we are is largely determined by who we believe we are.*

Now there is an important distinction to be made. Our individual meanings and narratives are important to us, and many of us share larger meanings with other people. However, having or believing a narrative doesn't necessarily mean that the narratives are true. The meaning we attach to Time is valid because we believe it, but it does not mean it is true objectively.

For example, I can believe I am the greatest tennis player ever, and this would be important to me and influence who I am, how I act, and the decisions I make. However, just because I believe this narrative and meaning does not make it true.

Again, the point being made here is that meaning is subjectively attached to Time. *We attach meaning to our Time using our minds.* Despite the bias inherent in this meaning, it is incredibly important to each of us and central to the experience of being human. But, at the same Time, this does not entail any sort of objective truth most of the Time.

Our lives are both meaningful and meaningless. Life is meaningless, because, at the grandest scale, we are subject to the influence of entropy and the arrow of Time, dictated by the 2nd Law of Thermodynamics. The future is composed of possibilities and probabilities—some that don't even exist yet and are unforeseeable.

But life is meaningful because we exist, and by existing with healthy brains and minds, we attach meaning to the events that happen to and around us. We believe this meaning and the story that emerges from it. Even so, this meaning changes over Time as we, and everything else, change.

Meaning is embedded into how our brains and minds are currently designed to process, perceive, and create our subjective experiences of Time.

7 Objective (Cost-Effective) Ways to Improve Your Subjective Experience of Time

---

If you want to become physically stronger, you'll need healthy habits - like going to the gym. You'll also have to give up unhealthy habits - like eating junk food. Building mental strength requires healthy habits - like practicing gratitude - while also giving up unhealthy behavior, like giving up after the first failure.

— Amy Morin

---

1. Drink a lot more water each day.
   We are in a constant state of dehydration as it takes water for us to function and live each second. Being hydrated also improves cognition and helps all parts of your body improve in function.

2. At least once a day, breathe out loud on purpose. Conscious breathing helps regulate heart rate variability and reduces stress on the body, brain, and mind.

3. Consistently use your off hand to do mundane chores.
   The act of learning new things or doing familiar things in new ways helps your brain stay active, improve cognition, and helps you learn about your own body.

4. Be genuinely kind to others.
   It will make you happier and make it easier for others to treat you kindly. How we interact with humans greatly outweighs other factors in how we enjoy life.

5. <u>Consistently document 3-7 things you are grateful for.</u>
   Gratitude is vital for reduced stress, more positive thinking and less negative thinking, better relationships, and much more.

6. <u>Question your values and beliefs every few months.</u>
   If they are valid, then you will learn why; if they are not valid, then you have the chance to shed them and adopt new ones that serve you better. Your values and beliefs largely influence your unconscious behavior and thoughts. Most of your Time alive is going to be unconsciously spent.

7. <u>Walk, exercise, or be active consistently.</u>
   As with your mind and brain, if your body isn't used consistently, it will deteriorate far more quickly. As a whole, you function with more efficiency and enjoyment. Your brain, mind, and body all have different needs to satisfy in order to function well as "one" conscious being.

Creating Purpose:
Starting with the End

Read Time: 33 minutes of attention

"Man is a goal seeking animal. His life only has meaning if he is reaching out and striving for his goals." — Aristotle

---

Aristotle was the one who educated me on the importance of purpose. I would highly suggest reading some of his work. He was and still is one of the greatest minds to push humanity's collective knowledge; and most of modern humanity has grown from his and other past great minds in some way. Not all of his ideas and work hold true today, but much of current knowledge grew from his foundations.

Purpose and meaning are similar ideas and definitely overlap in many areas. However, purpose is a useful tool for determining "right" and "wrong". If we know what our conscious or unconscious purposes are, we will have clearer ideas of what is right and wrong in a certain context.

Purpose is also useful for how we should spend our Time, and it is at the core of "smart-work". By questioning the purpose of something, we question a few things depending on the context. If we question a person's purpose, then we are questioning their goals and intentions for their actions.

If we question the purpose of a company, then we are questioning why it exists—its ultimate goal(s) that it exists to serve or achieve. Keep in mind these goals are not always at the forefront of the decision-makers of that entity and can lead to a large gap of what actually is done in reality, as compared to what should be done.

If we question the purpose of a goal, then we are questioning whether the strategy is worth spending future Time and energy achieving. Questioning the purpose of your goals can prove to be incredibly useful. Depending on the nature of the strategy and resources available, having a clear sense of purpose can save immense amounts of Time, stress, and energy.

Sometimes years can be saved and reallocated in one decision. Careers, marriage, pets, lawsuits, and other common occurrences are examples of decisions that influence how we spend years of our one future.

Using purpose, we look into the future and work backwards. From an individual perspective, we can learn to create and update our life purposes over Time.

What does it even mean to have a life purpose(s)? Well, by now, it should be clear that "life" can be substituted for "Time". So the question now becomes a little easier: What is the purpose of our Time spent?

As we move through life, our sense of purpose changes, because we change and our contexts change. So many other things can affect our visions of the future. Some people are able to create a purpose so strong and long-term that it becomes the driving force of how and why they spend the rest of their life.

But most of us do not have an idea of what we want to do with our entire lives. It's not fair to be asked to know that. But it is important to know on a smaller scale what your purposes are. In one form we have "New Year's resolutions", but even understanding our purposes for the month or the week or the day is powerful in terms of efficiency and enjoyment of Time.

I will share a few of my life purposes that determine what direction I will be moving towards as I approach the future.

Suresh's life purposes, as of 2.16.19:

- To live a happy, meaningful, and purposeful life (sets direction for my entire life, while giving me flexibility to be spontaneous in the moment as well)
- To raise awareness and educate humanity on the concept of Time and to help society and individuals value Time properly (sets direction for at least the next 30 years)

These are a few of my long-term purposes. Of course, I have shorter-term goals that also influence how I spend my Time, but those shorter-term goals/purposes are aligned with the ones I have shared.

Another important aspect of purpose is that it helps set direction and velocity as we move through Time. Regardless of whether you are aware of it or not, you are moving in some direction at some speed through Time.

In this way, we are all on an "autowalk"—one you would find in an airport that transports you in some direction without you having to actually walk or expend much energy. Our current society and culture is so obsessed with speed and efficiency that we have largely forgotten that where we are going matters far more than how fast we get somewhere. It doesn't really make much sense to go fast, if you don't have anywhere to positive to go.

Even if you are at a point in life where you are wandering, you still have a purpose in that your ultimate aim is to find yourself or explore the world.

In business and personal life, direction must be determined first before speed can become a factor to pay attention to. We can best take advantage of our technology and ability to move quickly, if we first determine our purpose(s). Otherwise, we are prone to quickly ending up nowhere or somewhere we don't want to be.

Be very cautious of making the pursuit of money or making material objects, your primary purpose for too long of a Time period. Those are usually ego driven desires and are usually placeholders for deeper happiness, meaning, and more fulfilling purposes we desire from Time.

The pursuit of money or ego-related things can undermine our own sense of happiness by neglecting the importance of our human relationships and/or our own self growth. Worse they can fool you into undervaluing Time and overvaluing money or any of its manifestations we can sense (gold, cryptocurrencies, etc.).

By consciously being aware of purpose, we partly address our "raison d'etre"—our reason for being. Why did you wake up today? Why do you spend your Time the way you do? In this perspective, purpose can become our compass through all the uncertainty we have to face in our lives.

Our purposes that we establish help give our Time direction and meaning—the feeling that we are moving toward something in the future and that we are not just a hamster running in place.

In a very real way, purpose influences the possibilities and probabilities we encounter and experience, the decisions we make, the people we interact with, and even how we perceive good/bad and right/wrong.

Time vs. Money

Read Time: 30 minutes of attention

"Every day is a bank account, and Time is our currency. No one is rich, no one is poor, we've got 24 hours each." — Christopher Rice

Way too many people, especially leaders in business and politics, use and misinterpret the saying, "Time is money". They think that it is describing that the value of Time is equivalent to the value of money. The idea that money has an equivalent value to Time is simply wrong, self-destructive, and over Time environmentally destructive.

No one in their right mind would value money over life. There may be certain moments where money can take a value that is equivalent to life, but these are usually rare life-or-death situations depicted in movies rather than in real life.

To illustrate the value of Time vs. money, we will use a simple mental exercise:

- *Please name something you can do without money.*
- *Please name something you can do without Time.*

If you are having trouble thinking of something you can do without money, here are a few activities to jog your mind: going for a run, playing with friends, spending Time with family, thinking, having sex, drinking water, being with your children, etc.

Now, if you are having trouble thinking of something you can do without Time, it is because you are asking your mind to think of reality that you would never experience. There is nothing you can do without Time, as far as the mind can understand.

Here's another way to look at this. A part cannot be greater than the whole. So, if life is the whole, then money is clearly a part. Some other parts along with money would also be work, happiness, family, travel, ambition, health, etc.

So, it doesn't really make logical sense to value the idea of money over the idea of life. Now the same goes for money and Time. Time is equivalent to life—in that life, in its entirety, takes place within Time. It's mostly commercial advertising, delusion, or ego that influences a person to value money over Time or life.

The thing that is confusing is that it is true that "Time is money". However, we can't forget that Time is many things. "Time is life" is also true. But the idea that the value of money is equivalent to the value of Time, is destructively incorrect.

In business, the phrase "Time is money" can be relevant in that cashflow does determine, to a large degree, whether a business has the ability to survive or not. But, again, business is only a part within the larger whole of life, so it's crucial to be able to step back and change perspective.

Getting this valuation between money and Time wrong, hurts yourself—specifically, it hurts your present self, future self, and your unconscious behavior. Eventually, it also hurts the people and environment around you. It feeds your ego rather than your sense of meaning, purpose, or happiness.

If you value money over Time, even unconsciously, you are more likely to make career choices that lead to unhappiness. In the decision-making process, you are paying attention to the wrong factors—ones that do not influence your future sense of happiness. You are less likely to judge that career choice based on what you would actually be doing with your Time, who you would be spending your Time around, and who you would be spending your Time working for. Those are the criteria that are more insightful toward how happy you would be in a job or situation.

Unconsciously, when valuing money too highly, you are likely to engage in comparisons and treat people according to how much monetary wealth they have in relation to you. In this way, it is nearly impossible to treat the janitor with the same human respect as the CEO. Even more importantly, it's nearly impossible to judge yourself with proper respect in relation to the janitor or CEO. In one comparison, you may be far superior; in another, you are far inferior. This isn't a controllable nor consistent way of judging yourself or anyone else.

However, if you value Time over money, your unconscious decision-making processes change, over Time. All people have Time, and this makes it easier to treat all people with equal human value.

Of course, our value is *different,* based on our personalities, occupations, passions, backgrounds, and more. The janitor and CEO are simply people that bring different, but necessary, value with their Time. In this way, every human has the same, but different, value.

There are many other indirect and long-term effects that come with properly valuing Time vs. money. One of the last ones I will mention is the ability to influence your sense of happiness, meaning, and purpose in life. This doesn't mean that your ability to grow monetary wealth is inhibited; it is actually enhanced to optimize to your unique personality, strengths, responsibilities, ambitions, and realities.

Ultimately, if you cannot value Time properly, you're making life harder than it will already be. How we value Time, consciously or unconsciously, influences how we value just about everything else including ourselves, our relationships, and even life itself .

The Point of Diminishing Marginal Returns of the Pursuit of Money

Read Time: 26 minutes of attention

"Money often costs too much."
– Ralph Waldo Emerson

According to a 2-year-long study conducted by Gallup, "Peak happiness costs between $42k-$120k", depending on where you live (in America). Money is of course important, and it has practical value. However, like almost all things, it has a point of diminishing marginal returns.

One major factor depends on where you actually live. Each country is different, depending on how cities or towns are designed and the in-general cost of living (food, housing, water, transportation, healthcare, etc.).

Even in each state in America, the cost varies. In California and New York, the point at which money becomes a non-factor to human happiness is around $85,000. In Nebraska, the point of diminishing marginal returns of the pursuit of money is much lower, due to the much lower costs of living in general.

It isn't wrong or inherently bad to make or possess millions or billions of dollars, but it should make you suspicious that there are billionaires that are unhappy. In fact there are plenty of examples of extremely rich and unhappy people and families all over the world.

Where the harm comes from is believing that money above your geographical threshold is going to add to your happiness. So if you just happen to be really good at what you do or have an ambition or passion that by definition requires larger scale monetization, then the flow of money will sort itself more naturally, based on how people want to spend their Time. For example, Bill Gates and Warren Buffett didn't set out to be billionaires; it mostly happened as a byproduct of the value they created for humanity in their own unique ways.

For those who believe that money can buy your happiness, you are right, but you need far less than you think. After you've secured that initial layer of security, the rest of your happiness becomes about how you spend your Time and the way you perceive and treat yourself, other people, your relationship to nature, and the world around you.

Money does help attain a certain level of freedom—freedom to do things. With money, we can pay to travel, take a vacation, satisfy unnecessary desires, do things with our friends, or simply wander. However in order to do anything, we must first have the Time to do it. It doesn't help to be a multi-millionaire that feels bound to their work every waking moment of their day. You may have the money to do whatever you want, but you don't have the Time, and thus you don't actually end up doing anything fun or exciting.

It is our greatest hope, and weakest ability, to have and use free Time. Money helps increase the probability of having and using free Time. This is the modern version of the old American Dream. Free Time is far easier to attain and influence given automation and the ability to work remotely.

If you're making more than $120k anywhere in America, and you are unhappy, it is probably not a matter that can be solved by attaining anything tangible or external, outside of your own mind.

It is most likely a matter of how you are spending your Time, who you are spending Time around, and/or why you are spending Time the way you are.

For some, that means moving from the financial industry and becoming a teacher. For others, it is simply perceiving your relationship to work and/or money differently.

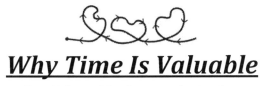

Why Time Is Valuable

Read Time: 25 minutes of attention

"Time is free, but it's priceless.
You can't own it, but you can use it.
You can't keep it, but you can spend it.
Once you've lost it, you can never get it back."
— *Harvey Mackay*

There is a large, significant difference between acknowledging Time as valuable and understanding its value. To understand the value of Time means to have it sink into your mind and brain and to alter the basic operating systems of your unconscious mind; this is where positive, sustained change occurs.

Time is finite for each of us, as individuals; it will end at some unknown point in the future. Plain and simple, this is why Time is valuable.

Unfortunately, many people do not value Time, until they are about to lose it, or someone close to them has lost it. The value you get from this book hinges on your ability to value Time without the need for a traumatic event. I urge you not to wait for a near death experience or the death of a friend, family member, or pet to value Time properly.

Time may or may not exist from a physics perspective. It actually doesn't even matter if Time does or doesn't exist from a physics standpoint—much in the same way our day-to-day lives wouldn't be affected if atoms turned out to not be real. Atoms are operationally important on a layer of reality we do not regularly work with or experience, for the majority of us.

Time, however, bridges all layers of reality. It is simultaneously relevant at the layers of atoms and particles and at the layers of humans, mountains, and ideas.

All humans need and use Time to function and have some sense of order in life, and even animals and trees have senses of Time. I'm not sure what that does from a physics perspective, but it can be seen as a successful evolutionary ability that has helped us individually and collectively thrive into the dominating species we are today.

Time is valuable to each and every one of us in a similar way that "life" is important to each of us. The entirety of our lives take place on a "sheet" (you can use any metaphor you like) of Time, and without its passage, we could not exist, as far as we know it. Time allows us to exist and is also the underlying reason why we will eventually die.

Some people have a positive view towards Time; some people have a negative one. I have found the most stable position to take is a neutral and objective one. Time is simultaneously your friend and enemy. Misery, boredom, and happiness all stem from our relationship with Time.

As far as our minds go, Time is crucial to understanding ourselves, the world around us, other people, culture, and life itself.

Your entire life takes place within the foundational structure of Time. Consider seconds, minutes, and hours that make up each of your days. That gets repeated day in and day out, without much variation. We also have days, weeks, months, and years to help structure past and future. All in all, it's pretty incredible how much of our minds and lives are embedded and dependent on some form of Time.

Even our unconscious brains and minds need and use Time. Actually, our subconscious, unconscious, and conscious minds are all influenced by Time on some level and to some degree.

This is important because the majority of our lives are spent unconsciously; actually, every second of our lives are spent unconsciously in one way or another.

We are not consciously operating underlying biological functions like the growth of body parts, shedding and growing skin, the beating of the heart, and many, many more operations that are necessary for survival and consciousness on a second to second basis.

Because we are always and constantly spending Time, we are all logically spenders of Time. Each and every living thing can also be seen as a spender of Time; the logic of Time does not discriminate. I see it as a great equalizer, because not only do we objectively spend the same amount of Time each day as everyone else, but we are also all similarly constrained and subject to the effects of Time that we all objectively spend.

Gravity is another equalizer in this sense, and we are all subject to its influence, whether we believe or are aware of it or not.

Like currency, Time can be spent and invested. When we learn to invest Time, we learn how to create and build higher levels of order. We learn that compound interest doesn't just apply to money. When we invest Time, we can grow happiness, monetary wealth, ideas, products, careers, families, meaning, purpose, ideas, and other forms of temporary order.

Socially, we can't collaborate or accomplish anything together without a common understanding of Time. Imagine you ask someone out for dinner. You both agree on Italian food and decide to meet at the restaurant. The inevitable question of *when* now obviously comes to mind. Without a common understanding of some form of Time, the date would most likely never occur.

The whole scenario loses a sense of order that we are familiar with in everyday lives.

To sum it up, Time is valuable because it holds, *at a minimum*, the value of life itself. Time is valuable because it is the underlying cognitive structure through which we perceive reality and ourselves.

Pasts, Presents, and Futures

Read Time: 2 minutes of attention

"People like us, who believe in physics, know that the distinction between past, present, and future is only a stubbornly persistent illusion."

– Albert Einstein

Technically past, present, and future are all the same thing. They are just cross-sections of Time, depending on where you measure in Time and on what scale. If you don't measure Time, then it is one entity or just one really large present moment.

However, by simply existing, we are measuring (subjective experience). Memories and expectations are based on the structure of Time, as we don't remember the future or predict the past. But it's important to understand the difference between them, because as humans, we have to move through Time, linearly and facing one direction. This means we must deal with past and future Time differently.

Conceptually, they are one and the same, but for humans, they serve different purposes based on our orientation within spacetime. The direction in which Time flows has already been discovered by science, in the 2nd Law of Thermodynamics. It moves, and all of our subjective experiences of Time move from past → future and are constrained by this aspect of the universe in which we exist in.

Past(s)

Read Time: 20 minutes of attention

"We are denied the ability to change the events that have occurred. We are also denied the ability to know with 100% certainty why things played out the way they did. However, our minds are embodied with the power to change the meaning of our past. Despite our human limitations, we are as powerful as we ever need to be."

– S.E.

The past is unchangeable, in the sense that the actual events that occurred cannot be altered or changed. However, the past is not the same thing as history or memory. History is not necessarily objective truth; it's a story, or collection of stories, of the past, created and recorded by humans.

History leaves out a lot of what actually happened—whether on purpose or by humans not being able to record/account for every second that has ever passed. Sometimes, history is fabricated so that one truth is lost and another "truth" is put in its place.

History tries to record a collective past, while memory helps us record our individual pasts. However the concept of history wouldn't really make sense without the idea that there are multiple pasts that connect to make up larger pasts, which connect to make up an all-encompassing Past. You can imagine this as the tributaries of a river merging together into the same river and eventually merging into the ocean.

Memory can be quite uncertain. Our brains were not built to be able to remember every second that we spend; it's simply too much information to process and store. We also do not have the focus to be aware of each passing second. So we chunk together blocks of Time around events or moments into experiences.

There are 86,400 seconds that pass each day. Most people are only consciously aware of a few of those moments passing by. Try describing what you did yesterday. Most likely you have to describe a few things that you did that day: "Woke up, ate breakfast, went to work, ate dinner..." *Your memory is also constructing a story, and this story is primarily built for cohesiveness, not truth.*

Now, if it is difficult to recount how we spent *all* our Time just yesterday, consider years ago or even back to your childhood. Much of that earlier Time spent is not accessible to your conscious mind today, although I'm sure technology will change that at some point in the future. But, for now, most of those moments are recorded somewhere in the subconscious brain and mind. Just because you cannot access them does not mean they aren't influencing you today.

Memory is fragile, and it can be biased when not taken care of properly. Even people who actively work on their memory are prone to misremembering, and as we age, our memory deteriorates at a fluctuating rate.

Despite the uncertainty of our memory, we can still use it to reflect upon the past to improve our futures. Just keep in mind that sometimes our memory will provide us with bad data and acting on that bad data can lead to bad decision-making. It's far better to admit when you aren't sure if you remembered something with a high degree of certainty (or low degree of uncertainty). Again this brings to light to our need to be familiar with uncertainty. In one way it is constraining, in another it's freeing.

Here is the positive and empowering part: *Our minds can change the meaning of our pasts.*

It is common for people to experience difficult childhoods, especially turbulent relationships with their parents. When we are teenagers, that period of Time feels and means something entirely different than when we are 40 years old, *looking back on it.* The events didn't change, but their meaning and effect on us can and does change.

There are some very important and powerful takeaways from this. First, we have power over what our pasts mean to us, especially so at an individual level. Second, sometimes we cannot know what something means, until enough Time has passed and we have had the chance to look back in hindsight and reflect on the event and seen what outcomes it eventually led to.

And lastly, and possibly the most immediately important, is the past may hold objective truth, but our ability to know objective truth is extremely limited. We must learn to reflect upon the past, our pasts, with integrity and uncertainty in mind.

The Present Moment(s)

Read Time: 20 minutes of attention

"Yesterday is gone. Tomorrow has not yet come.
We have only today. Let us begin."
— Mother Teresa

To reiterate: the past, present, and future are all connected. All pasts, presents, and futures are connected somehow someway.

The present moment is defined by our awareness. For most of us, the window lasts between 300 milliseconds and 4 seconds. Once we have defined what our present moment is going to be, we can then know where past and future begin. This relationship is very intangible, and this is where a lot of people get into trouble.

Without understanding or having defined what the present moment is, it becomes far easier to get lost in the past or the future. And, from earlier, we know that our minds are not constrained like our bodies. So it's very easy for our minds to be floating between past, present, and future without really knowing it.

The first step is to define the "now" that then determines where past and future start. Mindfulness and yoga suggest to us to connect our present moment with our own breaths. There isn't necessarily a wrong or right way to define your present moment. What is important is that you do define it and leave enough room to be adaptable to what your environmental influences are. For example, your present moment (your experience of it) will be different in the context of New York City as compared to Hawaii.

This process of "being" is also influenced heavily by the information we intake with our 5 senses, but also by our values and beliefs that we consciously or, more likely, unconsciously hold. Even when we are fully aware in the present moment, we are only able to pay attention to a sliver of reality that is shifting around us. Let me explain why.

Our eyes, ears, skin, nose, and tongue intake information that is then processed by the brain. This process is inherently limiting. Our "sight" in the present moment offers the most certainty we could have, and even then, we don't quite approach 100% certainty most of the Time. Light can play tricks on the eyes. Mirages and optical illusions are a few examples. We can compare this to our "sight" in the past and future, which are called *hindsight* and *foresight* respectively.

Our eyesight in the present is limited because we only have a defined visual range with our eyes, and we can only see on a small interval of the color spectrum. Our hearing extends only so far, and we can only hear at certain spectrums of sound. Additionally, we can only touch, taste, and smell what directly interacts with our skin, tongue, and nose. We are extremely limited in how we can interact with the world with our bodies.

Bats use echolocation and dolphins use sonar—abilities humans cannot naturally engage in—to interact with layers of reality that are very real. Certain birds have far better vision. The variety of ways life engages with the universe is much larger than we, being humans, understand or acknowledge on a day-to-day basis. Reality can be perceived in a variety of ways, through a variety of sensory organs.

Despite our limits, we still have some degree of power or influence, but never are we in full control. The present is where we have the highest degree of immediate influence. The opportunity to act and react opens in the present moment, and for humans, life unfolds one present moment at a Time.

However our first task is to define what our present moment is for ourselves. How we choose to define and interact with the present moment largely influences the reality we are going to perceive, believe, and act upon.

Future(s): The Realm of Possibilities and Probabilities

Read Time: 30 minutes of attention

"The best way to predict the future is to create it."
– Abraham Lincoln

Just like the past and the present, the future holds uncertainty as well, but it's a different kind of uncertainty. Instead of not knowing "what was", in the future, we don't know "what will be". This is obvious, but very important.

When dealing with the past, we must act like detectives sticking to events in sequential order as much as possible. When dealing with the present, we must play like children, fully engaged in what we are doing. And, when dealing with the future, we must think like professional poker players, with rules, patterns, and probabilities in mind.

The way I have come to understand it is that the future holds a near infinite amount of possibilities. Almost anything _could_ happen at any future moment, and the number of possible outcomes drastically increases the further you move out into the future from where you are measuring. A possibility can be pretty much any outcome or event that has even the slightest most absurd chance of occurring.

The interconnectedness of Time is so intricate that an event can be mathematically impossible only a few seconds before it actually happens. And that leads me to my second point: probabilities.

Quantum mechanics shows that we cannot predict with 100% certainty what *will* occur, only that is possible to calculate the probabilities of what *might* occur. This is why probabilities help determine direction and what most likely occurs over Time.

Let's use an example to illustrate:

Currently, it is 5:45am and raining outside. I predict 5 minutes from now I will still be laying in my bed writing this book; I would say its 99% probable. Why can't I say 100%? Because of the many possible, yet improbable outcomes that may occur within those 5 minutes. My dogs could scratch at the window and demand my attention; I may have to go to the bathroom; a fire could start; or an Earthquake could occur (San Andreas fault line isn't too far). While it may sound ridiculous, uncertainty must be accounted for; otherwise, we lose our ability to adapt to reality. It becomes a little more obvious in the next example.

Example 2:

Currently, it is 2019, and I am living in Sacramento, California. I predict that in 5 years I will be living in Austin, Texas. I would say it's 20% probable. In 5 years, damn near anything could happen that would throw off my prediction of living in Austin. I could get a job that takes me to New York; I could meet a woman and stay in Sacramento; the Stock Market could crash the economy; some new law could be created that prevents me or convinces me not to move to Austin; or climate change could rapidly make the state of Texas uninhabitable and force large migrations of humans to other parts of the country.

I have no idea what the probability of these outcomes might be; that isn't necessarily the important part. What is important is to realize and *take into account the large amount of uncertainty that is inherent when trying to predict the future, especially when you consider years out* into the future.

There are a million more possible outcomes that could prevent me from living in Austin. Some are more probable than the others, and none of us have an idea of what will actually happen until it gets closer and closer to 2024. I did not mention death as a possibility and probability, but that is one obvious possible outcome in which I would not be able to live in Austin in 5 years.

You would also have to keep in mind that, in 5 years, it's possible I do end up moving and living in Austin. Just by stating the goal, I am influencing the probability that it will occur, but there are too many factors outside of my control that prevent me from knowing or controlling that outcome with 100% certainty.

The rapid pace of change in tech and artificial intelligence adds to all this uncertainty. To look 2 years out is incredibly uncertain, because technology changes at an exponentially fast pace (Moore's Law).

Accounting for that, also keep in mind the complexity of interactions that occur on the internet, political conflicts, climate change, etc. It can get pretty overwhelming to realize how much uncertainty we actually are surrounded by. That's not even mentioning the daily interactions of people all over the world that influence and impact the changes and uncertainties that we cannot predict fully, but still must account for.

We don't need to be mathematicians, nor do we need to be too specific. Approximations and estimations are very useful when looking to the future. In this way, we can both plan for the future and be adaptable to change and disorder that inevitably comes with the passage of Time. Remember, while we cannot predict or control the future, we can influence it.

The Flow of Human Life

Read Time: 14 minutes of attention

"The ebb and flow of daily life can lead to wonderful highs, crushing lows, and everything in between."
— Julie Foudy

We, by nature of being human beings (Homo sapiens), are spenders of Time. We spend our Time consciously and unconsciously. However most of our Time spent on Earth is spent unconsciously. It could even be argued that every single second of our life is unconsciously spent, as we do not have conscious control over many of our bodily functions, nor did we consciously choose to create or grow them over Time.

Even when we are fully "present" and engaged in flow, we are only paying attention to specific parts/areas of a larger and fuller reality. When we are fully engaged in playing a game, we are paying attention to the rules, and there isn't enough Time to, in the same moment, also be consciously aware of our gut or the connective tissue in our knees. Most of us don't even have conscious access to most of our motor control processes, even if we wanted to. Our unconscious self underlies all of our moments, literally, in one way or another.

Another way this can be demonstrated is that when we are reflecting on the past or letting our mind wander away from the present in any manner, we are thus forcing our unconscious selves to operate our present selves.

We cannot simultaneously pay attention to the past and the present. So if you are having a conversation with a friend and your mind starts to wander to an event that happened earlier that day, your ability to respond and interact with your friend is greatly reduced because your attention is now in the past as opposed to the present.

These unconscious processes are common characteristics of human bodies, brains, and minds. What I mean is that while your subjective experience of life is unique, *your* body, brain, and mind, through which that experience takes place, is not unique.

Biologically, psychologically, and sociologically, there is a noticeable pattern to the life of a human being, just as there is to everything that persists through Time.

We all start off as babies, who are completely dependent on others to help and take care of us. Then we move to adolescence, teenage years, adulthood, old age, and eventually death. That is roughly the pattern we will follow over the course of our lifetimes, assuming we are living between 70-120 years.

If you think about it, each week, month, and year are literally the same thing categorized into different intervals for human use. Who is to say that we are not living out the same day, but our perception makes us believe that we are experiencing a different days? Structurally, there is no difference between yesterday, today, and tomorrow.

But our focus here is not on Time itself, but the human experience of it. So it is important to know that we experience Time locally. As we move through different stages of life, we experience Time differently.

We go through Time, though, from our subjective frame of reference—one present moment after another. This forces us all to be navigators on the "sea of uncertainty", with limited, but temporarily renewable, Time and energy.

While our pattern and long-term trajectory through Time is not unique, our subjective experience of the whole thing is. This leads me to one of my theories about the flow of Time, especially as it relates to human life.

Disclaimer: This is a theory and not to be believed easily. Test it against your own life and see if it holds true.

Theory: The flow of Time is not simply moving in a linear direction from past→future. Time is also not simply circular, but *I propose that the human movement through Time is simultaneously linear and cyclical.* In fact, I think humans move through Time in a spiral fashion.

We move through Time cyclically, but we experience Time linearly. The pattern of every human that has ever lived has roughly followed this pattern, yet no two people will have the exact same pattern. Going back to this idea that we are all similar and unique simultaneously. The ups and downs of life, your life, are depicted roughly in the unevenness of spirals and loops. Life is hard because we have to live subjectively and linearly, even though that isn't necessarily the case in other aspects of reality.

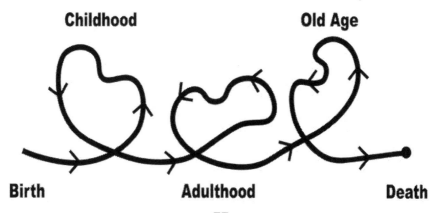

Childhood   **Old Age**

Birth   **Adulthood**   **Death**

The Importance of Timing

Read Time: 27 minutes of attention

---

*"They say, timing is everything. But then they say,
there is never a perfect Time for anything."*
– Anthony Liccione

We know Time as this ever-present "thing" that is also flowing seamlessly and continuously in the background of everything. But Time is not stitched together perfectly; there are many imperfections in the interactions of timescales that make the idea of "perfect timing" nearly impossible to achieve or predict.

Whether in business, social relationships, planning a vacation, or anything in between, you are forced to account for the phenomenon we know as timing. Either you take it into account, or you become accustomed to consistent failure and suffering.

Timing has implications in our biological functions, like sleep, diet, exercise, energy, and even cognitive performance. So much of our daily life is governed and influenced by the concept of timing. Studies have shown that the closer we structure our daily routines around the cycles of the Sun, the more likely we are to have positive mental, biological, and physical health over Time. It sounds simple, but in today's reality, it isn't. We have artificial light, smartphones, and platforms, like Netflix, that pull us away from nature's timescale and away from our natural optimal health.

Timing is also incredibly prevalent in our social realities. The difference in outcomes between going to a bank at 2am vs. going at 11am is dramatic. In the former situation, the doors are locked, and you might be considered a criminal. At 11am, the doors are wide open, and you are considered a valuable customer. The difference is *when* you go.

Another situation in which timing governs success or failure is our interactions between people. The success of asking a girl out, asking your parents for something, or securing a business deal is largely influenced by the accuracy of our sense of timing.

If someone is in a bad mood or just had a negative experience, it probably is best to wait until a later moment to ask them for something. This is obvious and built into our evolutionary social behaviors; we know this, whether or not we are aware that we know it. However, we, as a species, can be far better at timing in our interpersonal interactions. This does require a sense of empathy and connectedness as well. We cannot be great at timing if we are only concerned with ourselves or what is going on in our own minds.

Timing can influence us in other ways as well. For instance, beginnings and endings influence our mindsets and how we spend our Time. When we first start a job, we are much more excited with the little nuances, like having a fully stocked kitchen or the relationships we build with our new coworkers. Over the course of Time, we become used to these things, usually during the "middle" of our tenure.

When we transition to new jobs and approach our end at our current jobs, our mindsets shift, and we again notice the little things or become consciously grateful for the people that are around us.

Beginnings and endings can give us a new sense of energy and motivation, and this phenomenon provides the opportunity to mold and change ourselves and create or break habits.

Another common example is the difference between Sunday and Friday. Objectively there is no difference, they contain 24 hours of Time and that's it.

But as humans we attach meaning, so that Sunday is usually less desirable because it means the start of the week is near, and Friday holds much more positivity because it usually means that the end of the week is here and the beginning of our weekend is starting.

Interestingly, in another sense, one study found that a high percentage of marathon participants were 29, 39, and 49. Approaching the end of a decade influences us to consider what we did with our Time, and a large portion of people seem to think they didn't accomplish meaningful things in the last ten years. Apparently, training for and completing a marathon helps fill that void.

I could go on and on about how timing influences and governs our everyday lives and perceptions of reality. You can greatly reduce stress, suffering, and failure in all areas of life by becoming better at aligning and accounting for timing in all aspects of your life.

Stress Management and Time

Read Time: 22 minutes of attention

"There is more to life than increasing its speed."
– Mahatma Gandhi

Time and stress have a very dynamic relationship. It's a balancing act of allowing enough good stress to create a sense of urgency to get things done and to grow personally, while not overwhelming ourselves.

Too many people over-exaggerate stress in their minds, causing negative stress on their bodies, brains, and minds. This negative stress, over Time, can cause debilitating mental and physical medical issues and, in many cases, can influence the probability of death directly or indirectly.

Often that negative stress is completely made up in your own head. Even though the stress is largely imagined, our physical bodies can be impacted and feel the effects of that perceived stress. Our thoughts impact our brains, while our brains also impact our thoughts. We experience this negative stress in lower energy levels, unhappiness, unhealthy eating habits, depression, use of drugs, lack of exercise, and many other common symptoms of over-stress.

In general, people are starting to understand that too much stress, consistently over Time, will result in bad outcomes for your mental or physical health, usually both. What people aren't realizing is that stress isn't the problem itself; our perceptions and inability to see different or new perspectives are the problems.

Most people who feel stressed or over-stressed have been trapped into a certain mindset and are unable to see things from a larger or longer perspective. I see this a lot in the workplace.

Employees and leadership teams tend to over-exaggerate the importance of what they are doing in their own minds.

For example, I once worked at an ad tech start-up. My manager did not like the fact that I wouldn't take my laptop home after 5pm or that I refused to do company work on national holidays. I still did good work, met every deadline, and was getting better each day. But I wasn't going to give away my precious free Time just for the appearance of working hard. Not only that, none of what we were doing was saving or ending lives.

Sometimes it is necessary to spend some extra hours finishing a project, but that shouldn't be the norm. Otherwise, what were all the hours spent at the office for?

What did it really matter if our client didn't get an update on July 4th about how well their advertising campaign was tracking? In my manager's mind, there were dire consequences for not bending over backwards with our customer service. However, in reality, the consequences were minimal, if there were any. Most of the Time, clients didn't even appreciate the extra effort. Worse, they began to expect it, rather than be grateful for it. Keep in mind this mentality is more relevant today than it was 50 years ago, as cultural values shift.

Some people see work as a part of their lives, and some seem to view work as their lives. It is a subtle difference, but it has a big impact on how we manage our stress levels over Time. Doing good or great work does not require you to be over-stressed. I would argue that a human's best work comes when they have just the right amount of stress.

The nature of work is changing rapidly due to automation, cultural changes, and globalization. People are no longer seen as just tools for achieving monetary profit; we are human beings that need to, by nature, cultivate good physical and mental health for our own well-being and highest productivity.

Almost ⅓ of your life will be spent working. If your relationship with your work isn't put into proper perspective, you will more likely allow yourself to become over-stressed in your mind, which will cause far more physical and emotional suffering than is needed.

If you are a leader or manager, please realize and take the Time to understand that the culture you create at work influences every employee's sense of stress over Time. And if you are an individual, please realize and understand that stress can be good and bad. Negative stress is usually self-exaggerated in the mind, and if not addressed, chronic stress can kill you over the course of months and years.

Beware though, stress can occur in many areas of life, not just work. Unless it is a true life-or-death situation, don't let your imagination or fear run wild and cause unnecessary stress. Sometimes, it's hard, but with awareness and practice, we all can improve our ability to manage our own stress.

Our human relationships are another big cause of stress. We affect other people greatly, and it is easy to get lost in our own imaginations of what someone else may or may not be thinking or feeling. It is vitally important to foster and cultivate good friendships so that we can deal with our stress together, rather than alone.

The best defense against stress is to simply and purposefully breathe in and out. Going through Time will be hard enough, don't make it harder than it needs to be and definitely do not attempt to go through Time alone.

A Few Types of Freedom

Read Time: 38 minutes of attention

"For to be free is not merely to cast off one's chains, but to live in a way that respects and enhances the freedom of others."

— Nelson Mandela

Everyone has their own version of freedom, and America is a country built on this enticing idea. However, I think many people have an unrealistic idea of what freedom should be or is. The current understanding seems to revolve around the idea that freedom is the "ability to do whatever you want, whenever you want".

If that is your definition of freedom, then you are in for a miserable and caged life. Whether you want to believe in science or not, we are all bound by the laws of physics and the laws of the universe (the ones we know and don't know). There are always restrictions and rules that govern what we can and can't do at any given moment in life.

Space and Time are the first constraints that we must deal with throughout our lives. Other constraints in this realm include gravity, the need for rest and water, as well as the need to go to the bathroom.

Then, there are the less real, but strongly believed, rules that society abides by. These come to us in the form of constitutional laws, policies, rules, and social norms.

As children, most of us have strong desires to have the freedom to do things, especially things that we know we can't or aren't supposed to do. This includes the freedom to go play with our friends, to eat candy, to do whatever it is our parents said we couldn't do, etc. Even as teenagers, this idea of freedom to do what we want persists—drinking before the legal age of 21, driving faster than the speed limit, using phones during class, or cheating on tests, for example.

As adults, it starts looking more like not having to pay taxes, to not being monogamous, to being able to do illegal or partially legal drugs, etc. These fall under the class of "rule breaking".

We can also want the freedom to travel or go to festivals or sports events—all of which require both Time and money. Up to a certain point, money is incredibly important in securing freedom to do things.

(Here, I should mention, we can be happier with far less than we think, and we really only need enough money to cover our survival needs costs before the amount of money we have becomes a non-factor to our happiness.)

"Freedom from" is a little bit different—not better or worse, just different. This idea of freedom comes from understanding that rules and constraints are inevitable and that the best we can do is choose the rules and constraints that we are bound and freed by. For example, a person can desire to be free from anger, free from negativity, free from debt, free from anxiety, or free from fear. Many immigrants that have come to America desire to have freedom from oppressive dictators and have freedom governed by U.S. law, rules, and social norms.

As we age and get older, our perspectives change and we realize that rules aren't bad. They actually serve a good purpose: rules help create order.

Of course, there are good rules and bad rules, but in general they are designed for consistent types order. How could millions of people interact and get what they need to get done if not for basic written and believed rules of society?

During a Sacramento Kings NBA game, various rules apply to various groups of people simultaneously. The basketball players are subject to the rules of the game of basketball. The fans are subject to rules that do not allow them to walk on the court and to treat each other kindly (or not to engage in violence), plus seating rules, food rules, etc. Both fans and players are subject to the rules of the NBA, State of California, and the United States of America. When you think about it, it's pretty incredible how much the mind takes into account without us even realizing it.

Rules are mostly upheld because there are consequences, and I believe this is where human freedom starts. In my understanding, freedom is actually about knowing the rules and consequences that are governing you at any given moment or over Time, and acting and making choices within those set of rules and consequences.

The more you know about those rules, the more opportunity you have to be free. If you never understood the importance of math, physics, biology, history, sociology, or language, this is one of the main reasons why they are so important.

In order to authentically choose things, you have to first be aware that you are making choices. Once you get down to it, each second that passes is an opportunity to exercise freedom. Even in the most dire situations, you still have the opportunity to choose how you think, react, or perceive. In some contexts, it's much harder to bring yourself to that realization, but a reaction can always be a choice.

This is extremely hard to keep in mind, and most people struggle with it today, because we have little to no awareness in the present moment. Smartphones and apps encourage us to forget our freedom to choose, and instead we unconsciously scroll through our feeds allowing the app to make our decisions for us.

If you are not able to bring and hold your awareness in the present moment, then the unconscious mind and brain become the primary decision maker. Both are trained by the rules of our DNA, our cultural backgrounds, childhoods, and habits. It is far easier to be a cognitive slave to a well-established advertising brand or profit-first designed app than it is to engage in the power of your own free will.

I think *freedom from* has largely been neglected, and it is something people deeply desire. Given the direction humanity is headed, where attention is the highest measurable and monetizable commodity, maybe besides potable water and Time, *freedom from* things is the idea of freedom we will all need to become aware of and cultivate in order to be a happy and peaceful species.

Because in large part, freedom is the ability to do what we want, within what we should and can do. The path to this kind of freedom is first understanding the natural and cultural constraints on our bodies, brains, and minds.

The State of "Being Great"

Read Time: 20 minutes of attention

---

*"The greatness of a man is not in how much wealth
he acquires, but in his integrity and his ability to
affect those around him positively."*
– Bob Marley

Greatness is a concept that a lot of people strive to achieve, whether it's in sports, business, philanthropy, or life in general. Some of the most commonly accepted people that embody or personify greatness today are Roger Federer, Lebron James, Serena Williams, Tom Brady, Michael Phelps, and Kobe Bryant. (I am biased because I am male and grew up playing sports. I looked up to male role models for the most part, but there are just as many great females out there if not more.) I would also include figures like Abraham Lincoln, Martin Luther King Jr., Oprah Winfrey, Warren Buffett, Bill Gates, Albert Einstein, Mother Teresa, Gandhi, and many, many more who would not traditionally be recognized as "great" in the way it is commonly used today. Unfortunately, I am forced to leave out the vast amount of great teachers, mothers, fathers, doctors, friends, and more "ordinary" cases of greatness that go unnoticed in media and culture.

I think it's important to mention a few cautionary factors when it comes to the idea of greatness. First, it is possible to be great and be a bad person. People like Hitler achieved things at great scale. We must be very careful about blindly pursuing greatness; otherwise, we may end up hurting other people, rather than adding positive value to their lives. Greatness cannot truly be great if it is not first *good.*

It seems, really, that greatness is more of the ability to do something well consistently over Time, and improve. Only after a certain period of Time will people start to recognize your efforts as "great". (If you're accomplishing things for the external acknowledgement, you probably should reconsider how and why you are spending your Time the way you are.)

Second, greatness is not a solo journey; it is a collective effort to achieve a shared goal. It always requires the Time, help, and energy of other people. Even in solo sports, like tennis and swimming, greatness can only be realized through team effort. Michael Phelps may have won more gold medals than most countries have, but without his trainer and parents, he would not be who he is today.

Tom Brady receives the attention and spotlight, but a quarterback can't really do much if his offensive line can't protect him, not to mention the defense and special teams, which he isn't even a part of. They all affect the outcome of his greatness, and yet are out of his control. It requires trust, belief, mutual understanding, and practice between many humans.

Third, every single person can achieve some level of greatness by simply striving to be the best they can be and adding positive value to other people. Especially in today's world, we are going to need great teachers, great doctors, great friends, and, in general, great human beings. This changes the conversation and practice of greatness, from doing extraordinary things to doing ordinary things extraordinarily and consistently.

Lastly, greatness is not something that is achieved and completed; it is more of a habit of being. By waking up at 4am every day for years to practice, Kobe Bryant cultivated a sense of greatness within himself that was only recognized by others at some later point. To individuals like Kobe, greatness and the enjoyment of being great is more in practice (journey) rather than just in the outcomes.

In this way, a father can be great by consistently being there for his daughter's dance recitals, or a friend can be great by consistently being dependable and honest.

Consistency, by nature of the word, implies that something is done over the course of Time, not just once, but repeatedly and predictably.

We all have the opportunity to be great in our lives, whether we are positively adding value to humans, nature, things, or ideas. Please remember, though, in choosing to cultivate greatness, you are demanding the help and Time of others; and when you are recognized for your efforts, do not forget those who helped make it possible. Only together and through consistent goodness can greatness be cultivated, individually and collectively.

The Law of Attraction
+ Quantum Mechanics

Read Time: 28 minutes of attention

"I attract to my life whatever I give my attention, energy, and focus to, whether positive or negative."
— *Michael Losier*

The law of attraction is a widely known phenomenon. It illustrates that what we consistently think and believe is what we attract or manifest into our lives and/or experience of life.

Quantum mechanics is a little less intuitive. One aspect of quantum mechanics shows us that we cannot accurately predict the future, because when we measure it, we are influencing the outcome.

There are simultaneously several possible outcomes that could or could not occur, and as soon as we have measured for an outcome, we have interfered with the system and affected the outcome altogether.

(It can get complicated quickly, and in simplifying , I am nervous that I am compromising the integrity of these concepts. My goal here isn't to be perfect; it is to create a bridge between high academic knowledge and everyday life.)

So how are the law of attraction and quantum mechanics connected? I believe it has to do with the idea that when we measure for an outcome in Time, we influence the probability space that surrounds the outcome that we are measuring for.

95

Consciousness, simply existing as a living thing, is a form of measurement. Our thoughts, words, and actions are influencing the outcomes we experience in our realities. So, if our thoughts are negative and our self-talk is also consistently negative, we began to influence the outcomes that we perceive. We start to see and experience negative outcomes that are aligned with our initial measurements of past, present, and future. Reality is so massive and encompassing we can pretty much pay attention to anything that supports our previous beliefs, opinions, and biases.

By speaking and thinking things into existence, we are measuring the past, present, and future. By measuring the past, present, and future, we are influencing the outcomes we measure for. In quantum mechanics, we cannot predict the future perfectly, because in doing the measuring, speaking, and thinking into existence, we are influencing the outcome.

Now this would be a lot simpler if we were dealing with just one human being in a closed environment. But in reality, we are dealing with many humans, systems, and forms of consciousness that influence outcomes and, thus, make even predicting our own futures impossible.

This points to another feature in quantum mechanics called entanglement (the vast complexity of interconnectedness of nearly everything directly or indirectly in Time), and it gets confusing very quickly, especially when considering things at the layer in which particles or atoms are interacting. Nonlinearity becomes an important concept in understanding the complexity of entangled interactions. Instead of going further though, I will let you do your own research or let experts take the concepts further.

Using our brains, minds, and Time, we can and are influencing the future of the world. We do this simply by existing and being conscious.

I think Steve Jobs was hinting at this to some degree when he said this:

> "Life can be much broader once you discover one simple fact: Everything around you that you call life was made up by people that were no smarter than you and you can change it, you can influence it, you can build your own things that other people can use. Once you learn that, you'll never be the same again."

The point he is making is that we are simultaneously living in a world that was created by people, processes, and sheer chance, long before we ever born, and we are also co-creating and influencing the world and the future in which we and others will eventually occupy.

Every single person's thoughts, words, actions, and predictions of the future have possible influence on each other, our own selves, and our futures.

Leadership and Management in the Era of Automation, Climate Change, and Globalization

Read Time: 24 minutes of attention

"Leaders instill in their people a hope for success and a belief in themselves. Positive leaders empower people to accomplish their goals."

– Unknown

Leadership is going to be, and pretty much already is, one of the most influential aspects of the future of society—especially so in the business world.

In the past, western culture considered "business" leadership to be the medium through which we squeeze out productivity from employees and the environment. As automation becomes more prevalent and reduces the amount of Time it takes to create and build things, the purpose of business leadership must shift in order to cope with these changes.

Leadership and management are no longer two different categories, but they are very much the same role with different levels of influence. It is no longer sufficient to treat employees as if they were tools to achieve a goal.

Try getting any millennial to do a job by simply telling them what to do without a why behind it. Baby boomers who hold most of the leadership and management positions are increasingly feeling the pressure to change their leadership styles and cultures they create, because people want to be treated as if they are humans and as if their lives and their Time is valuable. This is becoming a demand more than just a request.

The equation is different now; it used to be productivity = number of hours worked. Western culture has become so obsessed with this idea—the idea of speed. However, *direction* is showing itself to be far more important than speed. Leaders must now follow the equation productivity = (enjoyment+efficiency of Time). In other words, we are shifting away from hard work, and success is increasingly becoming a product of smart work.

Another important aspect of leadership/management is the understanding that by positional nature, a leader influences the Time of other humans, by directing how they spend their Time and what the outcomes of their work Time should be.

Leadership is a responsibility and a privilege to influence the lives of other human beings. Bad leaders and managers can negatively impact employees' stress levels, sense of self-worth, productivity, and sense of meaning or purpose in life.

Many firms, businesses, and people still think that productivity is the result of brute force of hours put in. This is another idea that is losing traction as it becomes less useful in a fast paced world of technology, automation, and artificial intelligence.

No human can be productive for 12 hours straight, especially in today's world, where anyone can barely focus on one thing for more than a few seconds. Purposeful rest is critical for maximum productivity. Also, those who think that they actually worked for 8+ hours are most likely lying to themselves. We literally fool ourselves to uphold a narrative and outward appearance that we are hard workers; there have been plenty of studies on this. (In Laura Vanderkam's book, *168 Hours: You Have More Time Than You Think*, she dives deeper into this misconception)

Working 8-12-hour days isn't as productive as you'd think. Now this is definitely contextually dependent, and for those who are starting companies and are under life-or-death deadlines, it can be necessary for successful outcomes.

But, in general, for the majority of the workforce that doesn't operate under life-or-death deadlines and also have the use of technology or automation, it's far more productive to engage in smart work. Especially when workforces are split across the globe, across different Time zones and with different focuses and specializations.

It pays to be purposeful and to account for the fact that we are all humans who need rest and that we actually are more productive in the short and long term, when we enjoy what we are doing and who we do it with.

Whether you agree with this or not, this is the larger trend that we are seeing as more and more millennials enter the workforce, as globalization becomes more prevalent, and as the structure of life becomes more influenced by technology and automation.

So then, leadership, in today's and tomorrow's world, *is more about the ability to align an individual's sense of meaning and purpose with their team and the entity that employs them*. It is more about setting direction and finding ways to optimize efficiency + enjoyment of Time, individually and collectively.

Lastly, it's about building a sense of community between people from all over the world and collaborating in the same physical spaces or remotely.

Relativity, Time,
and Subjective Experience

Read Time: 40 minutes of attention

"When you sit with a nice girl for two hours you think it's only a minute, but when you sit on a hot stove for a minute, you think it's two hours. That's relativity."
— *Albert Einstein*

Time is both objectively and subjectively relative (flexible). For instance, Time flows at different rates at sea level than at the top of Mount Everest. Time also can be slower or faster for you and me, depending on our contexts. You and I can also experience Time similarly, even though we are subjectively measuring it separately. For example we both can feel like a week was "long", even though it has the same length of every week that has ever passed.

I am simplifying these concepts, but I am doing so in order to show how they are related to each other. I am not an expert, so take what you read here with a grain of salt and only believe what seems to hold true in your experiences consistently.

Einstein's Theory of General Relativity pretty much states that space and Time, spacetime, are curved. At the layer we operate on, this seems very odd since we cannot perceive this curvature of spacetime. But like atoms, this layer is the foundational layer upon which the realities we interact with. In fact, space is more like the surface of the sea, in that it oscillates, vibrates, and is affected by matter around it.

Earth has a massive density and "sinks" into spacetime. Gravity and the rest of the underlying forces more specific to Earth are influenced in this way, including Time.

Earth actually slows down Time and allows for the world we know. The closer you are to the Earth's core, the slower Time flows *objectively*. Earth Time is local to Earth, as Time on Mars does not flow at the same rate.

Relativity from another perspective is also the idea that each measurer, or person, experiences Time uniquely to them. One of the many properties of Time is that it is elastic and can be stretched.

I don't think Einstein was just describing relativity in the quote above though; I think he was also describing a nature of subjective experience—subjective experience being each of our own unique experiences of the world, of Time.

So, as I've come to understand and what I am proposing here is that relativity and subjective experience are connected, possibly even paralleled, with subjective experience possibly being a subcategory of relativity.

It's the reason that two people in the same situation can have two different experiences. One week can feel like a long Time for someone, and it can feel very short for someone else.

One thing that I would like to point out again is that while there is a subjective experience of Time, there is also an objective side to this.

In the example above, the two people have different experiences of that one week, but objectively, they are both experiencing one week only. There are a lot of nuances that go into a deeper understanding, like the fact that there is "local Time" that we experience, that the concept of a week is a made-up concept altogether, and much more that we don't need to dive into here.

All we need to know is that our subjective experience of the world is relative to us and that we have some degree of potential influence over how we experience our Time spent. We also need to keep in mind that there is a measurable objective experience of Time that does or does not align with our subjective experiences. And so it is true that the day felt long or short to us, but it is also true that regardless of what we experienced, the day was the exact same as every other day that passed.

Putting Life and Death into a Long Perspective

Read Time: 16 minutes of attention

"Life and death simply, are points in Time."

– S.E.

The mind is a powerful and incredible thing. It not only helps us survive on a day-to-day basis, but we are able to perform tasks that go far beyond survival. One of these tasks is the ability to perceive the entirety of Time.

We can imagine being on the outside of Time looking in, and it can provide some interesting insights that can help us live our lives more effectively and enjoyably, despite having nothing immediately to do with survival.

From this different perspective, on the outside looking in, the first interesting thing we notice is that, in every case, life precedes death.

If we aren't careful, we might mistakenly think that life causes death. However, I think, at this point, the most we could say is that there is a correlation. Not only are we able to see that death follows life, but life and death are just points in Time from this zoomed out perspective.

To view ourselves in this way can seem a little cold and lifeless, but my goal isn't to convince you one way or another of something, but to show you a different perspective and let you decide for yourself what you want to take from it.

Personally, it helps me understand that I am a small blip on a much bigger radar and that I am part of something bigger; or sometimes it's just good to keep my ego in check. It can be easy to get trapped into the everyday grind of living and lose perspective on where we sit within Time. Some would simply call this mental exercise gaining perspective or stepping back.

Every once in a while, it is good to remember we are simultaneously living in a universe with atoms, black holes, galaxies, and other things far beyond our bodily grasp. Everyday stresses of work, interpersonal relationships, and anxieties tend not to have much power over us when observing them from this long and large perspective, if even for one minute.

Time and Music

Read Time: 6 minutes of attention

"I feel like music can affect you in so many ways. When you hear a song with a happy melody, it can change your mood; it can change your day."

– Kygo

If music can impact your day, then you have already felt one relationship that music and Time have. Music has an incredible power to help us influence how we feel and experience Time.

I listen to music almost every single day, for a significant percentage of the day, and I am pretty sure I am not alone in how much I listen and hear music, not to mention enjoy it.

Personally, I like to listen to all kinds of music. People listen to all kinds of music for all kinds of reasons. Music, in its great variety, helps bring a sort of harmony, rhythm, or order to our minds and bodies.

One of the foundations of music itself is Time. It takes on different names under this category of human knowledge. Within music, we know Time as rhythm, beat, tempo, synchronization, and other forms that are more specific to different methods of creating music.

It's also been shown that we can influence the biological and neurological states of a person by manipulating beats per minute and other aspects of tempo and rhythm. There are many health and enjoyment benefits that can be and already are being derived from this relationship. Before a sporting event or game, people listen to certain kinds of music to make them think and feel a certain way, and during a wedding we listen to certain kinds of music to feel a different way and so on so forth.

In contrast, we are sensitive to disorder in music. We quickly notice or become irritated by static or music that we do not like. Music has many relationships with humans, as individuals and as cultures.

I wrote this section not so much to go into the reality of how Time and music are connected, but to bring attention that they are interconnected, because music is such a prevalent and powerful concept across all cultures.

To show that Time underlies music is simply another piece of evidence of the reach and usefulness of Time.

The Compartmentalization of Time

Read Time: 40 minutes of attention

---

*"I chose not to care. And if it scared me at first how
easy it was to make myself feel differently about
something by simply deciding it,
I decided I could ignore that too."*
— *Greer Macallister, <u>Girl in Disguise</u>*

Time does not take any breaks; it flows seamlessly and continuously no matter what we are doing. In the morning, we can barely avoid a fatal car accident and then hours later be drinking a beer with friends; it may feel like two different parts of Time. But don't let Time fool you; it's all part of the same thread.

The human brain is not built to account for every second that passes, and we actually need to break up Time into categories or segments.

We need to act differently in different situations. For example, we act and talk about a certain range of topics with our friends and act and talk about another different range of topics at work.

Compartmentalization occurs when we categorize or separate something into different sections. We all do this with our Time.

There are positives and negatives to doing this, and I will highlight a few of each to help raise your awareness and empower you to optimize how you spend *your* Time.

There are plenty of categories and a variety of ways we break up our Time. For example, we have work, family Time, leisure, vacation, morning, evening, beginnings, endings, childhood, old age, and much more. By compartmentalizing our Time in these ways, we can induce the mindsets and energy we need to be successful in each category at the right Time.

The same mentality and energy that is required at the end of a basketball game with the score tied is not going to be desirable when you are laying on the beach in Hawaii. If you want to go crazy, then go ahead and treat every second of your life as if it was Game 7 in the NBA finals. But for most of us, there is a Time to be locked in and focused on achieving some sort of outcome, and a Time to simply relax.

A more common example is that the mentality, behavior, and language we use at work are not going to be effective when we arrive at home and are interacting with our spouse and kids. So compartmentalizing allows us to optimize our body, mind, and brain for different situations, interactions, and goals.

However, there are many dangers that can damage our lives if we aren't aware of the reality that Time flows continuously and seamlessly.

One of the big negatives is that we think it is acceptable to treat people poorly in one arena of our life and fool ourselves into thinking that it's not who you are because you treat people well in another area. Let me use the work and family example again to illustrate the problem.

If, at work, Charley treats his colleagues terribly because they are slow or not as competent as himself or, in general, he doesn't show basic human respect, then his employees will perceive him as an asshole and possibly a "bad" person.

But then work ends, and Charley goes home to his wife and kids. There he shows them love and patience. Or maybe it is the exact opposite, and Charley treats his coworkers with respect and patience and is an asshole to his family.

Because we need to chunk our Time in blocks, it can be easy to lie to ourselves and forget that all of our Time is connected. We can only ignore and suppress reality for so long before we are forced to deal with the misalignment of our thoughts, words, and behaviors.

From this perspective, each of us must walk a fine line between efficiency and delusion when we compartmentalize our Time.

Cultivating Mental Health

Read Time: 20 minutes of attention

---

*"You, yourself, as much as anybody in the universe,
deserve your love and affection."*

– Buddha

Warren Buffet described the importance of physical and mental health by using the metaphor of your body and mind as your only lifetime *vehicle*—a vehicle that uses water, energy, and Time and that has many compartments, which have different functions, such as a heart, immune systems, motor control, arms, skin, brain, and mind.

Logically, your mental health is going to be one of the most important factors on the quality of your life. Everything in our life flows through the brain and mind. It makes sense to invest the Time, energy, and attention into your own mental health.

There a couple common misconceptions that I'd like to address. First, mental health is not just a concern for people with mental illness; it is the concern of everyone with a brain and mind.

Second, good mental health, which gives you the best chance of experiencing a high quality of life, is not just the absence of mental illness, but the active cultivation of robust, positive "states of mind".

The quotes in the figure on the next page is from Carol Belgman's book, *Train Your Mind, Change Your Brain*, and it shows what I mean.

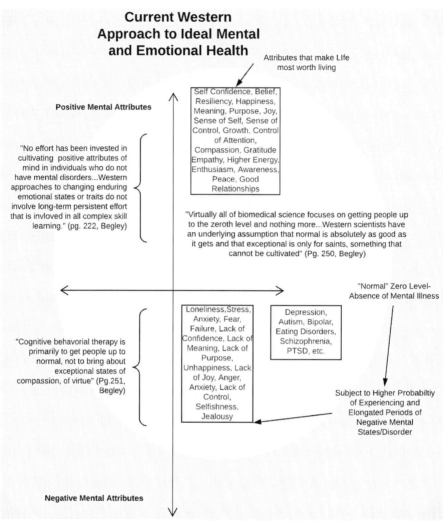

Current Western Approach to Ideal Mental and Emotional Health

Attributes that make LIfe most worth living

Positive Mental Attributes

Self Confidence, Belief, Resiliency, Happiness, Meaning, Purpose, Joy, Sense of Self, Sense of Control, Growth, Control of Attention, Compassion, Gratitude Empathy, Higher Energy, Enthusiasm, Awareness, Peace, Good Relationships

"No effort has been invested in cultivating positive attributes of mind in individuals who do not have mental disorders...Western approaches to changing enduring emotional states or traits do not involve long-term persistent effort that is invloved in all complex skill learning." (pg. 222, Begley)

"Virtually all of biomedical science focuses on getting people up to the zeroth level and nothing more...Western scientists have an underlying assumption that normal is absolutely as good as it gets and that exceptional is only for saints, something that cannot be cultivated" (Pg. 250, Begley)

"Normal" Zero Level- Absence of Mental Illness

Loneliness,Stress, Anxiety, Fear, Failure, Lack of Confidence, Lack of Meaning, Lack of Purpose, Unhappiness, Lack of Joy, Anger, Anxiety, Lack of Control, Selfishness, Jealousy

Depression, Autism, Bipolar, Eating Disorders, Schizophrenia, PTSD, etc.

"Cognitive behavorial therapy is primarily to get people up to normal, not to bring about exceptional states of compassion, of virtue" (Pg.251, Begley)

Subject to Higher Probabiltiy of Experiencing and Elongated Periods of Negative Mental States/Disorder

Negative Mental Attributes

Figure: Positive vs. Negative Mental States Approaches

The basis of mental health stems from trained abilities—specifically the *abilities to express and manage a range of positive and negative emotions*, the *abilities to form and maintain good relationships with other people*, the *abilities to cope with and manage change and uncertainty*, and the *abilities to learn and grow*. This is according to the Mental Health Foundation's definition of "good mental health".

We train our minds and brains by using, spending, and investing our Time—by making decisions that benefit us in the future when fully immersed in the present moment.

We already discussed how the passage of Time is correlated with entropy or disorder. While our minds are not bound in the same way our bodies are, both body and mind are subject to disorder. Disorder in the mind can manifest itself as lack of self-belief, anxiety, or unhappiness.

Without training your mind and brain (literally building and strengthening synapses that induce certain states of mind more than others), you are more likely to have these negative states of mind influence your perception of your own life. If you want to be physically healthy and active, then you must train your body consistently in order for it to perform and function well, the same is true for mental health.

That's another aspect of mental health that I'd like to highlight: We have a certain degree of control or influence over our mind and brain. In neuroscience, it's called *neuroplasticity*. Until recently, it was believed that our brains became fixed and that we were stuck with whatever we had after the age of 25 or so.

Modern research in neuroscience has shown that our brains have a high degree of neuroplasticity. Over the course of Time, our brains are adapting and changing. When we learn new things or do the same things in new ways, we reduce the level of disorder within our minds and brains and strengthen synapse interactions that increase the probability of experiencing positive states of mind.

Learning new languages is a great way to keep your brain young and active over the course of Time. You don't even need to go that far; for example, I use my off-hand to brush my teeth in the morning. Some people use their off hand to eat their cereal in the morning; it really doesn't matter what it is that you do, as long as it's different for you and requires some sort of engagement or flow within those moments.

What is important here is that when we consciously try new things or improve on our strengths and when we actively engage with our minds and brains, they perform better, and we are happier.

Why Bad Things Happen to Good People: The Second Law of Thermodynamics

Read Time: 20 minutes of attention

"Anything that can go wrong, will go wrong."
– Murphy's Law

Anyone can look up the proper physics version with a quick Wikipedia search. The simple version of the 2nd Law of Thermodynamics is this:

As Time passes in the direction of past→ future, entropy (disorder) increases within a system at some scale or degree.

Entropy can also be seen as randomness, chaos, or change, but what this means is that the nature of Time is *correlated* with disorder, randomness, and chaos.

Things are supposed to break down and go wrong. Now this is confusing for a lot of people, because when we look around with our eyes, we see a high degree of order. Our cities, roads, and furniture don't seem to be in a state of constant disorder. But if you believed everything your eyes showed you, then you wouldn't know much about this world or yourself. The key part of the above definition is "to some scale or degree".

Imagine that you just bought a new house on the beach in Mexico. My first question is, "Will the house still exist in that form a thousand years from now?" Probably not. Why? Because of many possible reasons. It could have been a poorly built house;

119

a hurricane could destroy it; someone else could buy it and remodel it; it could be destroyed in war; or it could accidentally catch fire due to a laundry mishap. There are near infinite amount of reasons why the house won't exist in the original form at some point in the future. These are larger level examples of entropy.

From a biological and personal perspective, stress can cause many issues with our bodies and brains. Health issues, usually, are the result of smaller scale disorders building up and eventually becoming what we know as heart attacks, liver failure, or other forms of medical emergencies.

Sometimes, these things occur out of sheer probability, but a lot of the Time, we exacerbate the problem, because our eyes and egos are fooling us and telling us nothing is wrong. So we rationalize to ourselves that it is okay to continue to excessively drink, smoke, or eat junk food.

Unfortunately, a healthy person with great self-discipline is still subject to unseeable deterioration. For healthy people, the probability is far lower that you'll need to pay thousands of dollars in medical expenses. An unhealthy person who has terrible habits is on a faster treadmill to death; but a person with the best mental and physical habits is on a slower and more enjoyable treadmill.

What is objectively important, though, about the 2nd Law of Thermodynamics is that it applies to everyone and everything within the Universe. Earth itself is subject to this disorder; and at some point, our planet will no longer exist in the form that we currently are familiar with.

The interesting thing about Time and disorder is that we actually use Time to create temporary order. What I mean by "order" is low levels of disorder. The device or book you are using to read these words has low entropy. Disorder is occurring at a slow rate within the device or book, so it could be said to have a high degree of order.

One way to view temporary order is to imagine an 80-year life. Probably around the age of 20+ is when we start actively building careers, families, and our sense of happiness. But I don't know anyone who has had a career with no mishaps or a family with no marital issues, or even an absence of sadness within an overall happy life. Furthermore, I don't know anyone or any career, family, or happy life that has lasted forever.

Life is hard for this reason. We have to constantly be investing Time, energy, attention, money, and other resources into building and sustaining our temporary order in our lives. It's a never-ending process, until our Time runs out.

Reality and Time

Read Time: 32 minutes of attention

"Reality is that which,
when you stop believing in it, doesn't go away."
— Philip K. Dick

There are many layers to reality, and Time connects all of these layers together.

Time is a foundational structure of all realities. This does not mean, however, that Time plays the same role in all realities, but that it does indeed play a role. We have the 2nd Law of Thermodynamics to thank for this knowledge. A few common examples can illustrate the uncertainty we have to deal with when dealing with a concept like reality.

Imagine a bus filled with people. After a few minutes, the bus starts to smell bad, and finally, one person exclaims that someone had to have farted. The only way to know who actually did it is for someone to admit it. Then everyone would simply have to believe and trust that it was actually that person; the other people wouldn't actually *know*.

One person claiming it was them doesn't say anything about whether or not two people had been the culprits. If we had the ability to truly know objective reality, we would know exactly who farted and when. But we don't have that ability, and so we must rely on each other to piece together our versions of reality to get to a closer image of objective reality, or actual truth.

There is an objective reality, separate from what you and I believe. It is recorded in the passage of Time—every second that

123

passes everywhere in the known universe. Our ability to know that objective reality is extremely limited. In fact, our brains are not designed to be aligned with objective reality.

Being humans, we love stories; we crave meaning; we forget the boring; and we see the world tinted with our biased and limited subjective frame of reference.

In basketball, a player gets called for a foul and immediately disputes it to the referee. The player claims he never touched the opponent. He may even believe it with all his heart and mind. But what *actually* happened?

Then the player looks up on the big screen and sees the replay, where different angles of the play are shown again, and he clearly slaps the opponent across the body. Despite his belief, he was wrong. His version of reality was not aligned with objective reality.

Unfortunately, most of our lives are not recorded, and so we are not able to simply look at a replay of how objective reality played out and adjust accordingly. We only have our individual and collective versions of reality, and that requires us to engage in belief, trust, and massive amounts of uncertainty.

Reality is a confusing concept for a few reasons. One is that reality is massive idea larger than any individual can possibly conceptualize fully. It extends much farther and deeper than we think—all the way from black holes to touchdowns.

Another reason is that there are many realities that we engage in on a daily basis without realizing it. There are no clear-cut boundaries; everything is blended together, especially the way we perceive the world.

Atoms, particles, light, the sun, humans, mountains, and energy are all aspects of an objective reality that simultaneously exist on different layers. They all exist right now for both you and me, whether either of us believes it or not.

A third reason is that our lives are now intermixed with made-up realities that are collectively believed. Yuval Harrari explains this well in his book, *Sapiens*. Money is something we all collectively believe and use on a daily basis, throughout the world, whatever form it may take. Money undoubtedly plays a role in my reality, as well as yours, and also in every other human's reality that doesn't live in complete isolation.

But money is not "real" in the same sense gravity is "real". If the human species were to go extinct, so would money, but gravity would continue on without skipping a beat. Yet for you and me, money and gravity are two concepts that interact in the same realities that we engage in on a daily basis.

So again, there are many realities that we engage. Some of them are actually real and based in the laws of the universe (physics); some are completely made up and believed by you and me; and some are believed by only you and not me and vice versa.

Ideally, all of us would try our best each second to stay as close to this objective reality as possible. It's the real source of truth that we desire to know.

But objective reality is cold and does not care for our hopes, dreams, nor our reputations. It simply unfolds second after second relentlessly.

Instead of facing and adapting to this cold objective reality, which actually gives us the most amount of power to influence the future, we lie to ourselves and others. Instead of admitting our mistakes, we say we did nothing wrong, or that it was someone else.

Why put our reputation and social credibility at risk when a little white lie keeps everything intact? No one can actually prove or know my wrongdoing, because their ability to know objective reality is extremely limited. This mindset is a slippery slope that gets a lot of people in legal trouble, in society and in business.

125

Going back to the first example, if no one admits to farting, then they won't be caught. Their social standing is not damaged. It can get dangerous quickly though.

In other situations or contexts, when we lie to others, we are first lying to ourselves. We separate ourselves from objective reality and delude our minds into believing another reality. Over Time, if we don't face reality and admit our own faults or embrace uncertainty, we can diminish our abilities to act and produce desirable outcomes that occur outside of our own beliefs.

Separating from reality forces us to live inside our own minds and makes it incredibly hard to engage in flow and enjoyable work or activities.

Staying close to reality is not necessarily a joy ride, however; horrible things can and do occur in the world every day. Sticking our heads in the sand is also not really an option; by doing so, we will quickly start to destroy ourselves, each other, and the world around us. Climate change, political conflicts, and other global risks are just some of what happens when we stick our heads in the sand and do not face and adapt to reality.

A Gratitude for Time

Read Time: 25 minutes of attention

---

*"Do you love life? Then do not squander Time, for
that is the stuff life is made of"*
– Benjamin Franklin

Of all the things I've learned in the last 4 years of researching the concept of Time, this has been one of the most important understandings:

All humans, all living things, share a "Gratitude for Time" because life ends at some unknown point for each of us. It is a universal cognitive foundation upon which to cultivate positive mental health while facing reality.

We all share a gratitude for Time, because as far as we can understand it, the passage of Time allows for our existence. Said in another way, we could not imagine ourselves to exist without Time passing. Since we live in this reality and we cannot change it, we might as well use it to our benefit.

Gratitude is a central concept to almost all religions, good health, empathy, kindness, and happiness in general. Gratitude is similar to being thankful for something. It goes further than just being thankful for something though; it goes into having an understanding of how and why we should be thankful for something, in this case, Time.

When we allow ourselves to be grateful for Time, a few things occur. First, we face the reality of death, and this then allows the individual to direct attention to what matters to them most, given the reality that their Time is finite. Throughout recorded human history, humans have verbally and tangibly expressed the deepest and strongest of desires to have a sense of meaning, purpose, and happiness from their finite amount of Time.

Throughout our individual timescales, good things, bad things, and boring things will happen to us. We cannot predict the future, nor escape death, but we can increase the probability of living happy, meaningful, and purposeful lives, individually and collectively.

It's a choice, among other things—a choice to view the events in your life as opportunities for growth and a choice to treat people kindly by being grateful for the experiences that you expected and didn't expect, enjoyed or didn't enjoy, and even the ones you remember or don't remember.

Even when someone treats you badly or unkindly, it can be a lesson of how to act more enjoyably or efficiently in the future around similar types of people or similar types of situations.

To be grateful for Time is a step in the direction of inner peace. In a weird way, it is a simultaneous acceptance of being powerless and incredibly powerful—powerless in the approaching certainty of death, and powerful in how we create meaning and influence the lives we live.

I'd like to be clear: This is not religious. Having a gratitude for Time is based on logic and on the probability of death. It's rooted in the 2nd Law of Thermodynamics and how the human mind understands and experiences reality. It is a verifiable concept or "truth". As sure as the Sun rises, we must accept our dependence on Time and use it to our advantage .

Personally, I think that having a gratitude for Time is a pathway to understanding the physics, math, and/or logic behind religious and spiritual practices that have brought positive value to billions of people throughout human history.

Part of the reason I think this is because neuroscience and psychology are already showing that Buddhism has verifiable neurological benefits. Gratitude has shown, over many years, to be incredibly powerful in changing the perception of our inner and external worlds.

Expressing gratitude also has neurological and physiological benefits in terms of our heartrate variability, levels of stress, perceptions of reality, neuroplasticity, and even brain activity associated with positive mental states.

The last thing I will leave you with is that this entire book is not about how you should live your life. My intention and, hopefully, my execution have been about raising awareness of certain issues that currently govern the modern human being and will govern humans in the future, in order to better face the global challenges pressuring our species and all life on Earth.

Having a gratitude for Time is something that exists, regardless of whether we choose to believe it or not. It is an opportunity to authentically live your life with a hint of positivity towards yourself, others, and the world around you, without fooling yourself. It connects us to our ever-changing selves, to each other, to other species, and to nature.

In other words, it is a process for facing reality each day, without losing our minds or losing hope. It takes our greatest fears, like death, and turns them into opportunities to create meaningful lives and mold the future.

~ The Beginning ~

References & Resources

Book Title	Author
Why Time Flies	Alan Burdick
Einstein's Dreams	Alan Lightman
Language, Truth, and Logic	Alfred Jules Ayer
Too Big to Fail	Andrew Ross Sorkin
The Idea That Is America	Anne Marie Slaughter
The Fountainhead	Ayn Rand
Imagined Communities	Benedict Anderson
The Conquest of Happiness	Bertrand Russell
Algorithms to Live By	Brian Christian, Tom Griffiths
Minding Time: A Philosophical and Theoretical Approach to the Psychology of Time	Carlos Montemayor
The Power of Habit	Charles Duhigg
How to Win Friends and Influence People	Dale Carnegie
When: The Scientific Secrets of Perfect Timing	Daniel H. Pink
Thinking Fast and Slow	Daniel Kahneman
This Is Your Brain on Music	Daniel Levitin
The Compound Effect	Darren Hardy
This View of Life: Completing the Darwinian Revolution	David Sloan Wilson
The Psychology Book	DK Publishers
Golf Is Not a Game of Perfect	Dr. Bob Rotella
Into the Magic Shop	Dr. James Doty
The Finders	Dr. Jeffery A. Martin
Why We Do What We Do	Edward L. Deci
High Growth Handbook	Elad Gil
The Goal	Eliyahu M. Goldratt and Jeff Cox
Devil in the White City	Erik Larson

The Systems View of Life	Fritjof Capra, Pier Liugi Luisi
Mind Gym	Gary Mack, David Casstevens
The Next 100 Years	George Friedman
The Practice of Creativity Through Synectics- The Proven Method of Group Problem Solving	George M. Prince
Live a Thousand Years	Giovanni Livera
Swim With The Sharks Without Being Eaten Alive	Harvey B. Mackay
World Order	Henry Kissinger
Reality Is Broken	Jane McGonigal
The Patterning Instinct	Jeremy Lent
Time Wars: The Primary Conflict in Human History	Jeremy Rifkin
The Way of the Champion	Jerry Lunch PhD
Good to Great	Jim Collins
The Ultimate Gift	Jim Stovall
Zen in the Martial Arts	Joe Hyams
Measure What Matters	John Doerr
The Man's Guide to Women	John Gottman PhD, Julie Schwartz Gottman PhD
On Grand Strategy	John Lewis Gaddis
The Construction of Social Reality	John R. Searle
Wooden on Leadership	John Wooden and Steven Jamison
The Happiness Hypothesis	Jonathan Haidt
How Not to Be Wrong: The Power of Mathematical Thinking	Jordan Ellenberg
The Power of Your Subconscious Mind	Joseph Murphy PH.D
Effective Listening	Kevin J. Murphy
The Fourth Industrial Revolution	Klaus Schwab
168 Hours	Laura Vanderkam
The Tipping Point	Malcom Gladwell
Meditations	Marcus Aurelius

Nine Lies About Work	Marcus Buckingham, Ashley Goodall
The Defining Decade-Why Your Twenties Matter and How to Make the Most of Them Now	Meg Jay Ph.D
Finding the Next Starbucks	Michael Moe
The Seven Laws of Money	Michael Phillips
The Consciousness Instinct	Michael S. Gazzaniga
Flow	Mihaly Csikszentmihalyi
The Time Keeper	Mitch Albom
The Five People You Meet In Heaven	Mitch Albom
Entrepreneurship for the Rest of Us	Paul B. Brown
Time and Narrative	Paul Ricoeur
The Essential Drucker	Peter F. Drucker
Managing Oneself	Peter F. Drucker
Managing for the Future:1990's and Beyond	Peter F. Drucker
Eleven Rings	Phil Jackson
Superforecasting	Philip E. Tetolock, Dan Gardner
The Acceleration of Cultural Change	R. Alexander Bentley, Michael O'Brien
Now, The Physics of Time	Richard A. Muller
Screw It, Let's Do It	Richard Branson
QED	Richard Feynman
Influence	Robert Cialdini
Can Democracy Survive Global Capitalism	Robert Kuttner
Playing from the Heart	Roger Crawford
How High Can You Bounce?	Roger Crawford
The Art of Possibility	Rosamund Stone Zander, Benjamin Zander
King James Believe the Hype	Ryan Jones
Train Your Mind Change Your Brain	Sharon Begley
A Brief History of Time	Stephen Hawking
The 7 Habits of Highly Effective People	Stephen R. Covey

Made in the USA
Lexington, KY
26 November 2019